act

ALIGN–CONNECT–TRANSFORM

"This book is amazing in its power, style, and profound simplicity. Cathy Brown has made the wisdom in this book so clear and understandable. A synergy of wisdom and elegantly simple yet profound powerful steps to create the life you want and desire! It will help many people overcome obstacles, align, and connect to their essence self. When I started reading "ACT, Align-Connect-Transform" I couldn't put it down!! Thank you for writing such a powerful book that is written in a simple, easy to understand language that everyone will be impacted, inspired, and be transformed from it!"

Evelyn Apostolou, C.E.O. and Founder, Quantum Edge Healing Institute.

If you are not yet familiar with the Universal laws that orchestrate and manage every act of creation, this book will provide an easy introduction, along with practical insights into how these forces are powerfully at work in your life. And if you're already a practiced deliberate creator, Cathy's five-step approach will deepen your understanding that the vibration you are offering in each moment is the invisible source of every event and circumstance that unfolds in your life, and show you how to more consciously offer that vibration. It's a valuable resource for everyone.

From the foreword by Christy Whitman, *New York Times* Best-Selling Author.

act

ALIGN–CONNECT–TRANSFORM

Discovering the 5 Foolproof Steps
to Create the Life You Want

Cathy Brown

Forward by New York Times
Best-Selling Author *Christy Whitman*

DEDICATION

To My Family ...

Mom and Dad (MaMa and BaBa), who gave me the love, support, confidence and courage to grow and succeed in life. They were my biggest cheerleaders in life and continue to be from behind the veil in heaven.

Andrea and Christine, my two beautiful, strong and independent daughters. I trust I played a small role in your development because you played a tremendous role in mine. You have become my #1 support system.

My fun-loving grandchildren: Toni Lin, Kaesyn, Maguire, Marissa, Ainsley and Mason. "NiNi" thanks you for just being you and making the world a better place.

I could never forget my "fur babies," my "collie family," past and present. Past: Bonnie, Flame, Stormy, Ruff, Ready, Shelby (my one Sheltie), Magic, Mikey, Mikey Man and Lexi; and present: Leo and Zen. You have taught me the true meaning of unconditional love. I can't imagine life without all of you.

ACKNOWLEDGMENTS

Throughout my entire life, I have been blessed to have family, friends, teachers, coaches and mentors loving and supporting me.

ACT Align-Connect-Transform, is my most recent creative adventure, one that I could not have completed without these following individuals cheering me on. The secure feeling that they all had my back gave me the confidence and determination to become a published author. Thank you all. Words cannot adequately express my love and appreciation.

To Andrea and Christine, my daughters: You are my life, my support system, you are always there, even through your busy family life. Thank you! You make me so proud, I hope I have returned the favor.

To my wild and wonderful friends: Linda Millisor, Pat Neidhart, Vinny Holdren, Carolyn Savikas, and all the Columbus Collie Club Members. This thing we call life would be so boring without you. Thanks for coming along on this ride with me.

To Christy Whitman, my mentor, teacher and coach: You came into my life at the perfect time. "When the student is ready, the teacher appears." You have guided my spiritual growth and confidence far beyond my loftiest expectations. You gave me a new direction in life filled with growth and self-love. My deepest thanks.

To Evelyn Apostolou, my beautiful teacher: You introduced me to the healing arts of Reiki and Hypnotherapy, but more importantly you showed me how powerful and loving spirit can be. Your love and light shines through all you do. Thank you for "softening" me.

To the Quantum Success Coaching Academy Team (QSCA): It is an honor to be part of your "Tribe." It is truly a Dream Team. Theresa Hoerman, Tammy Lawman, Susie Ennis, Nada Howarth, Julie Kleinhans, Rachel Christie, Janet Bieschke, Stacy Ison, Lola Love, Beth Myers, Barbara Anseimi, Sheila Callaham, and Tabitha Hamilton and Andrew Lawrence. I apologize if I missed anyone. You are all Goddesses. (Andrew, you are an honorary Goddess.)

To Ridgely Goldsborough, my WHY Mentor: Thank you for showing me the "WHY way." Knowing my true inner self has made all the difference. I am now able to understand and love myself so much more. I love being a WHY facilitator and sharing its amazing benefits with the world.

To the Self-Publishing School (SPS): Thank you, Chandler Bolt, and your entire staff for your expert self-publishing course, which made my first time writing journey a wonderful experience.

To Scott Allan, my writing coach: I gained clarity and direction from your continued guidance. I hope to follow in your literary footsteps. I'm so glad you were my coach.

I would also like to thank to my Book Launch Team for helping me introduce my book to the world. Your comments and guidance have meant so much. I could not have done it without your assistance.

Special appreciation to my creative support staff:

Photographer – Stephanie Bowen
Cover Design – Ida Fia Sveningsson Konsult
Editing and Formatting – Spencer Borup

And a last but not least, thank you, all my past, present and future clients and readers. It is always an honor to serve you.

"Let's Transform Lives Together."

FOREWORD

By Christy Whitman

We live in a culture that indoctrinates us early on in the notion that hard work, ambition, and persistence at all costs are essential components when navigating the road to success. And in fact, the book you are now holding in your hands was written by a woman who employed all of these qualities and more, and created a life for herself that just about everyone would consider successful. At a time when men dominated the world of finance, Cathy transcended both the gender gap and her modest beginnings to become a high-powered executive with a top New York investment firm, where she earned both prestige and a big paycheck.

But after fulfilling even her loftiest dreams, Cathy realized that the outer trappings of success did not have the power to create inner fulfillment, and began what has been a decades-long spiritual quest for the true source of happiness. What she discovered—and shares throughout this book—is that while action and effort can produce external results, the sense of internal contentment and satisfaction that we are all seeking can only unfold when we learn to harness much more subtle and powerful forces.

Cathy is a graduate of the Quantum Success Coaching Academy, which I founded over a decade ago. The

Academy has trained and certified thousands of people from all over the globe to become Law of Attraction coaches, who support their clients in deliberately creating the experiences they most desire and deserve. If you are not yet familiar with the Universal laws that orchestrate and manage every act of creation, this book will provide an easy introduction, along with practical insights into how these forces are powerfully at work in your life. And if you're already a practiced deliberate creator, Cathy's five-step approach will deepen your understanding that the vibration you are offering in each moment is the invisible source of every event and circumstance that unfolds in your life, and show you how to more consciously offer that vibration. It's a valuable resource for everyone.

Christy Whitman
Scottsdale, AZ
Spring, 2017

A NOTE FROM THE UNIVERSE

The truth is, you live in an infinitely kind and unspeakably wise Universe that you are a part of, not apart from; where you, yourself, are a creator. And of your countless creations, your life is one. You chose to be here. And infinitely benign and intelligent yourself, your choice was impeccable.

In this greatest adventure of all adventures, whatever you wish for is my command. I am your most faithful servant and constant companion. Whatever you once dreamed of for yourself, can still come to pass. It's never too late to come from behind, and things can literally change for the better in the twinkling of an eye—as you have so often shown us in the past.

You are a supernatural being whose thoughts become things and for whom all things are possible. This, being a creation amongst your own creations, is as good as it gets, because whenever you don't like what's before you, you can simply recreate it ... without hindrance from the past or so-called contracts you no longer remember. There are no other rules. There are no hidden agendas. And there are no unknown variables working against you in this paradise you call home, where manifesting change most certainly couldn't be any easier than getting what you think about.

Oh yeah, way better than winning the lottery. Huh?

The Universe

—Mike Dooley, Notes from the Universe, May 4, 2017
New York Times best-selling author

As a token of my appreciation to my readers,
I've got 3 Gifts for you

CLICK HERE to receive your FREE Gifts

http://lifecoachingbycathy.com/book-free-gifts/

Happy Thoughts Thursday
Weekly subscription to Cathy's weekly inspirational News and Notes filled with valuable ideas, quotes and affirmations to put a smile on your heart and assist you to create the life you want.

Manifesting Abundance Meditation
Please relax and enjoy this going within meditation, designed to reprogram for abundance.

7 Universal Laws Report
A summary report on the 7 Universal Laws showing you how you can transform your life.

CLICK HERE to receive your FREE Gifts

http://lifecoachingbycathy.com/book-free-gifts/

TABLE OF CONTENTS

INTRODUCTION

"Do not be afraid to walk the path that you must go just because you cannot see the end. The path becomes clearer as you continue to go on."
—Tracy Allen

How is your life going? Is it all you ever dreamed of? Deep down are you happy and fulfilled? Unfortunately, not many of us are.

Today, so many people are running around exhausted and depressed searching for happiness and fulfillment in all the wrong place. Ever felt that way? Well, you're not alone.

Bronnie Ware, who worked in a palliative care unit for many years, helping those who were dying, compiled a list of the most common regrets by the people she cared for. The #1 regret was ... "I wish I had the courage to live a life true to myself." Bronnie found, at the end of life, it became easy to see how many dreams and desires had gone unfilled. Most people had not honored even half of their dreams. That's sad ... and it doesn't have to happen.

Hope is on the way. Here is a fun little book with a big message to transform your life by aligning with your higher self and connecting with the Universe using five foolproof steps. Really! Create the life you want in five simple steps! Sound too easy? Well, life is supposed to be easy, and fun. No hocus pocus, just finding joy, love and fulfillment the easy way. It worked for me, and thousands, even millions of others, and it will for you too!

This book is designed for people who are failing in the "creating the life of my dreams" department. Stop that feeling of failure right now! I believe that there is no such thing as failure, only feedback to help you course correct and get back on your happiness track. Are you ready to get back on track? Then this book is for you.

I also used to chase my happiness, but even while making big bucks as a corporate executive on Wall Street, something was always missing. I discovered money doesn't always buy happiness, however, it can be a great side effect.

You see, I was looking for fulfillment in all the wrong places—searching outside, not inside. What? Yeah, searching outside—thinking that if I could only make my outside life change, my inside feelings and emotions would change too. Unfortunately, that's not how it works.

I used to say, "If only I could get that hot sports car, that great job, or that fancy house, then I would be happy." Ever think that? And, how did that work for you? For me, it bombed ... big time.

I got the hot sports car (a $60,000 Lexus SC 460, hard top convertible, silver with black interior), the great job (running two Morgan Stanley Stock Brokerage offices, with ninety brokers, thirty support staff and over $30,000,000 in assets) and even the fancy home (a beautiful four-bedroom, sprawling ranch home in an upscale subdivision, sitting on a half-acre of manicured landscaping with a screened in pool).

Yes, I had all the "trappings" I thought I needed to be happy, I had produced all the "stuff" to make me feel good, to feel that I had arrived, but something was still missing. I was working from the outside in—thinking if I just worked my butt off, I'll prove to everyone, especially myself, that I am worthy and deserving. Then I'll be happy by having all the material "toys" everyone associates with happiness.

WOW! What's wrong with that theory? Here are a few key problem phrases:

"Work my butt off"
"Prove to everyone, especially myself"
"Make myself happy"
"Have all the material toys"

Let me emphasize, there is absolutely nothing wrong with having a financially abundant lifestyle. In fact, I am a Creating Money Coach, so I love money as much as we all do. However, these trappings of success are just that: the "extras" that will follow your peace and fulfillment. The key is *how* you find your true clarity and joy. By living deliberately and creating "inside-out," you can then reach your full potential and happiness quota.

Now, as a Certified Law of Attraction Life Coach, Hypnotherapist and Reiki Master Teacher, I have found my answer, and I can't wait to share it with you! By putting my spin on the ancient metaphysical teachings, and sharing my life experiences, these principles are easier to understand and practice. These five foolproof steps have been successful for my clients and myself as well. You can put them into practice immediately and produce amazing results and start finding happiness in all the right places.

Here's my recipe ...

We start by understanding and strengthening your partnership with your higher self (God, or whoever you look to as your higher spirit), and finding clarity and focus on your desires, so that you are ready to take full advantage of the four Universal Laws (the Laws of Attraction, Deliberate Creation, Allowing and Detachment) to create the life you want. These laws are everywhere, they are eternal, absolute, exist and influence our lives whether we accept them or not. Since they are that powerful, it makes sense for us to know and understand them.

We then stir in a huge helping of trust and gratitude. Mix well, taking care, patience and practice to add the final ingredient, alignment-momentum. We keep stirring as we become one with ourselves and the Universe to move forward with our desires.

That's the Five-Step, Foolproof Recipe:

1. Clarity and Focus
2. Universal Laws
3. Trust
4. Gratitude
5. Alignment–Momentum

We can't forget the bonus, the icing on the cake, Discovering Your Authentic Self. This bonus ingredient may be the most important component, because if you don't know who you really are, how do you know if you are truly happy? Are you pleasing yourself or trying to please others? I bet we've all been there a time or two.

It all sounds great, right? But right now, I bet you are thinking W.I.I.F.M? That's an old sales acronym for "What's in It for Me?" Here's what's in it for you ...

By focusing on the enclosed principles, processes, techniques, my personal experiences and your commitment to creating your desired transformation, I promise, you will:

- Find clarity in what you want
- Feel a growing connection with your higher self and the Universe
- Discover how easy it is to work with the Law of Attraction
- Create financial abundance
- Know and live your true authentic self

- Find peace and fulfillment by finally taking control of your life

All from this little book? Yes, this little book and your sense of adventure and commitment. The results can be amazing. Transformation is not only possible; it's happening every day. Here's what a few of my clients are saying about the principles listed in this little book.

Anita, from North Carolina, says, "They took me further in my business in a few weeks than I had come in ten months."

Christine, from Ohio, says, "They opened my eyes to the power of positivity and creating the life I desire."

Mayda, from New York, says, "Thank you for helping me break through my limitations and issues that were not serving me anymore."

Are you ready to create the life you want? Are you ready to ACT, Align-Connect-Transform?

As we begin our journey together, thank you for allowing me to be your guide. Once you start working with these five foolproof steps, you will see results ... in not just in one, but many areas of your life. And ... to show my appreciation, I have a special gift for you in Chapter 11. Don't peek yet! Let's start becoming friends first as I share my life and the amazing direction it has taken thanks to connecting with the Universe.

Okay ... are your seat belts buckled? All systems go ... ready to fly? Ready to Align-Connect-Transform? Ready to meet Cathy Brown, your tour guide?

We don't meet people by accident. They are meant to cross our path for a reason. I am so appreciative we are crossing paths today. Let's discover our reason together.

See you on the inside.

Love ya,

Cathy

CHAPTER 1
My Journey, B.S. (Before Spiritual)

"Don't you wish you could take a single childhood memory and blow it up in a bubble and live inside it?"
—Sarah Addison Allen

Who is this Cathy Brown, and more importantly, why should you listen to her? Well, I am probably not all that different from you; maybe a little older, maybe a bit more experienced in creating, and I am always growing, just like you. These spiritual teachings that I am sharing have been with me my entire life, way before I realized what they were, just as they are and always have been with you. As I share my story you'll see how I was guided by these unseen, loving forces.

I came from where you are right now. Since I have recognized and adopted these principles, I have created the life I want, the life I had only dreamed about. If I can do it ... so can you! Let the introductions begin!

Hello, pleased to meet you, I'm Cathy! Actually, I was born Catherine Dorothy Diegler (after my Mom) on August 8, 1947 (a raging Leo astrologically), the only child of Albert and Catherine Diegler. Dad was a supervisor of Bell Telephone Laboratories and Mom was a stay-at-home mother, Brownie and Girl Scout leader, church volunteer and in charge of our three-bedroom, Cape Cod style home in Whippany, New Jersey. We were a solid middle class family. Dad was in total command, making and enforcing the rules while Mom often ran interference on my behalf.

Being a plucky little kid, always small and always loud, I was a tomboy at heart. I loved the outdoors and preferred to play with the boys climbing trees rather than with the girls playing with dolls.

I had a cousin, Eddie, who was five years older, who I would always tag behind like a little puppy. Anything adventurous he would do, I would copy—most times not so successfully. My arms and legs were constantly black and blue and scratched. I can't remember how many trees I fell out of, but luckily never broke any body parts. The Universe was looking out for me even then.

I remember one time having to get a tetanus shot after stepping on a rusty nail while climbing on a pile of old wood from a demolished house. That hurt! But what hurt more was hobbling home, leaving a trail of blood, while explaining to Mom and Dad how I could have possibly stepped on that nail in the wood pile that I was told not to play on over 100 times. I knew there would be hell to pay if I got caught on that woodpile, but it was such a fun adventure and all the neighbor kids were playing on it. I was beginning to learn about choices and consequences at an early age.

I was a happy-go-lucky child, totally in love with my best friend, Bonnie—a tri-color collie. As the story goes, Mom and Dad were thinking about getting a dog for the family. I was about two at the time and a co-worker of Dad's was a backyard Collie breeder, who recently had a litter of puppies. He asked Dad if he would like to bring the family to see the cute collie babies. Dad had heard that Collies were a great family dog, wonderful and protective with kids. He was soon to find out just how protective they were.

We arrived to see the puppies outside in an exercise pen. As soon as I saw those little fluff balls jumping excitedly all over each other, I squealed joyfully, ran at full speed (as fast as my two-year-old little legs would carry me), and shoved my arm right into the pen, almost giving Mom a heart attack.

The first little fur ball to immediately lick my arm became my first collie, Bonnie. That day was the start of my love affair with Collies, which is still going on today. (I'll explain more about that Collie-Cathy connection later in Chapter 11). I currently have two beautiful male collies, Leo (Sable and White) and Zen (Blue Merle) who are both sleeping nearby as I write. Bonnie and I were inseparable. I felt that spiritual unconditional love and connection with animals as a toddler. Bonnie became my best friend and protector sometimes to her detriment, as evidenced by the following event.

Just about a year after adding Bonnie to our family, I was sitting on my dad's lap as he was reading a book about a lion to me. Bonnie was peacefully sleeping at his feet. Out of the blue, I bit Dad on the hand (guess I was demonstrating my lion side). Dad screamed and raised his hand to smack me. But before he could make contact, Bonnie grabbed his arm, snarling like crazy. Poor Dad, being attacked by both his daughter AND dog! Well, as you can imagine, Bonnie and I were both punished that night. And as far as I can remember, that was the last book about wild animals that Dad ever read to me. He preferred to stick with less aggressive story lines.

My childhood was happiness personified; two loving parents, Dad was a little strict at times, but it was pretty much a "Father Knows Best" or "Leave It to Beaver" (sorry, I am dating myself) childhood growing up in the 1950s. That is until my first traumatic event.

While finishing 8th grade, Dad was suddenly promoted and transferred to the Bell Labs in Columbus, Ohio. I'll never forget my 8th grade graduation dance—holding hands with my first boyfriend, Robert, my new love, as he was so excited telling me all the fun we were to have this summer. Oops ... we moved to Westerville, Ohio the next week. My first lost love. Even though it was puppy love, it still hurts, right?

Off to high school in the Midwest. My love for sports and athletic ability made me think it would be an easy deal to become a cheerleader. It didn't quite turn out that way. I made the finals skill-wise, but learned a valuable lesson during the final competition ... Popularity and Marketing are powerful! If the kids don't know you (the new kid from New Jersey), they don't vote for you. I never tried out for cheerleading again, choosing to focus on other ways to make my mark. I joined all the clubs and competed on all the girls' athletic teams (the tomboy in me still lived) and even met my future husband. I was beginning to discover my true self. I liked being in charge, running things, not giving my control and power away to others.

High school was fun. I quickly learned what was required and ways to shortcut the process. I started to become more involved in organizing programs, enhancing my leadership skills, becoming a member of the National Honor Society and President of the Girl's Athletic Association. I skipped study halls to assist the Phys. Ed. Teacher.

During High School, I learned a limiting lesson: to never outshine your boyfriend. I joined a rifle club, because he had an interest in shooting. I didn't know the barrel from the butt of a rifle, but I figured how hard could it be? I guess not very ... because I won my first tournament and was awarded a shooting mitt. I was so embarrassed as I took my prize, having no freakin' idea what it was. But I did know what that look was on my boyfriend's face. It's okay to be good, if you are not better than him. Limiting beliefs were already creeping in.

On to higher education at Otterbein College (now Otterbein University), where I studied to become a Physical Education teacher. Living at home, attending classes during the day and working as Teen Club director on the weekends and continuing to spend summers as a playground director, I was always running the show while building my leadership and teaching skills.

I was planning my career and practicing my independence when my high school sweetheart (at the time, my fiancé) was drafted into the Army and was stationed in Europe, rather than Vietnam (thank you, Universe). We got married just before he left for Frankfurt, Germany and I followed six months later, not quite finishing college to my family's dismay. (I did return three years later to complete my student teaching and graduated with a Bachelor of Science in Education.)

Living in Europe was quite an adventure and right up my alley. For extra money to travel and "live it up," I worked as the Assistant to the Sports Director of the U.S. Army Special Services. The director was a young, single guy who enjoyed having fun and partying more than working. Once again, I got to run the show, overseeing the sports programming and gymnasiums for the entire battalion.

I had a lot of time on my hands while "supervising." Time well spent planning trips to Austria, Italy, Scandinavia, Spain, England, Ireland and all over Germany. I enrolled in German classes to better speak the language. "Ein Bier, bitter" and "Wo is die toilette?" Which became ultra-important, when at the tender age of twenty-two, I was introduced to German beer. It was nothing like the 3.2 crap we used to sneak in school. This was the high-test stuff that knocked me on my ass more than once. I still have a three foot Lowenbrau lion (I must have something with lions) as a memento, but I don't quite remember how I got him ... that's another story.

I experienced so many new adventures while abroad, always being open to my sense of adventure, wherever it would lead me. At that time, I could not explain the sense of protection and confidence I felt during my travels. I know now it was my partner in life, the Universe, keeping me on track and safely bringing me all the adventures I requested. Ask and you will receive!

After three years abroad Pete, my husband, our German Collie, Stormy, and I came back to the U.S. I finished my degree and secured a mid-year teaching position in the small country town of Mount Gilead as the high school Health and Physical Education instructor.

One of the reasons I think I got the job is that I brought home boxes and boxes of sports equipment to use in classes from my tenure in Special Services. Some of the

Army gymnasiums were closing and what were they going to do with all those balls and stuff? So, during my interview with Mount Gilead, I said, "Take me and you get all my balls ..." Well, maybe I worded it a little differently. Lesson learned—Always Repurpose Everything!

As a recent college graduate and a "sophisticated" European traveler, I was out to change the entire educational system. Girls were no longer going to be second class citizens in the sports arena. Remember, I had "all the balls" ... or so I thought. Although my heart was in the right place, my tactics left a lot to be desired. Saying that I ruffled a few feathers was putting it mildly.

I started a girl's gymnastics team and got the whole town riled up when I had the audacity to parade my gymnasts around in those "sexy" leotards. It probably didn't help to have the local preacher's daughter on the team.

Of course, there was no money for warm-up suits (to cover those skimpy leotards), because it all had gone to the boy's football and basketball uniforms. I kept being told we would have to vote on it at the next Parent's Athletic Association meeting, with the knowledge that the meeting would mostly comprise of football and basketball parents, and they would never endorse such an idea.

Did I mention that even though I was little, I was loud? I set my intention (I was using the spiritual principles without even realizing it) and personally called all my gymnastic parents, who in turn called all their friends and relatives. When the next Parent's Athletic meeting came, they needed many, many more chairs. And guess what? When the gymnastics warm-ups came to the floor for a vote ... we were approved. Imagine that!

My victory was short lived however, when the next day I was called to the principal's office and given a pretty severe dressing down for "stacking the meeting." Oh, yeah ... the feathers kept flying.

The next fall we were hosting the District Gymnastic Championships and needed to have a forty by forty foot floor exercise mat. The superintendent, by now not my biggest fan, told me they could not provide transportation of such a large mat because of liability. He thought that was the end of it. I heard that I needed to find other means to transport this monster of a mat. Guess they didn't know who they were dealing with, as I easily found some friends with a tractor trailer and it was delivered right on schedule.

My theory has always been "When there is a will ... there is a way." Even though I didn't know or understand the Law of Attraction, I guess I was using it. What you focus on, you bring to you.

Well, I continued to cause more and more "rocking the boat" events in the eyes of my superintendent. So much so, that I was told the school was not renewing my coaching contract the following year. I could return as the Health and Phys. Ed. teacher, but not as the gymnastics coach. This caused a near riot at the next School Board meeting as all my gymnasts and parents stormed the gates. All that was missing were the flaming torches.

I learned how hard it was to be the first woman to fight the establishment in a man's world. This was the 1970s! Going up against the "Boy's Club" took guts and yes, "all the balls." Valuable lessons were learned in how to ruffle fewer feathers while making politically correct improvements. Maybe slower changes, but more effective in the long run. Coming from a place of love and respect, the spiritual way, rather than ...I'll show you whose boss was a valuable lesson I was learning the hard way.

The timing was right for a change, anyway. I didn't want to stay teaching at Mount Gilead without my coaching—so the Universe stepped in with perfect timing (as always), and I found myself pregnant with my first child. Way to go Universe!

Andrea was born April 3, 1976, and my life was full of love. I enjoyed the time off watching Sesame Street over lunch and planning my next adventure, which was the birth of Mid-Ohio Gymnastics Academy in Marion, Ohio. No business training, jumping into the pool and in mid-air realizing, "Oh, crap—no water." I organized, taught and marketed the academy and my husband, Pete, worked full time as a computer tech and instructed in the evenings.

As all small business owners know, it was not a nine-to-five job. Our family lived and breathed gymnastics. Even little Andrea, then three years old, enjoyed "Mini-Stars" classes.

During our second year of business another bundle of joy came into our lives. Christine arrived on March 18, 1979. By this time, I had hired several instructors and was back to running the show, where I was happiest. I enjoyed the marketing and promotion more than the teaching.

But the Universe must have had something else in mind for me, as the local economy in Marion took a severe downturn and we sold the school to our head instructor. Pete returned to focusing on his computer tech position and I jumped into radio advertising at WMRN radio in Marion. Once again jumping into the pool, praying there might be some water this time. It just felt right. I was learning to trust my instincts without being completely sure why, they seemed to be leading me in a positive and abundant direction.

I had little actual sales experience, but I figured it out quickly by closing my eyes and asking for help. Amazingly, the ideas just came. Looking back, I am floored at just how much the Universe and the Law of Attraction were influencing my life without me even knowing it. When you ask for help, set your intention, it will come. And it did.

I soon became a highly productive salesperson with a gift of gab and an assortment of schmoozing techniques. I was having a ball, working long hours, and driving the girls to dancing, Brownies, sports events, you name it. I was so focused on my girls and career, going a hundred miles an hour, I could not see my marriage eroding right in front of my eyes.

We divorced the following year. Divorce is never easy and mine was no exception. Pete was a good man and father. We just started to grow apart, with different goals and desires. My focus was on the girls and my career, which left little time for him.

Looking back, the signs were there but I just didn't see them. If I had realized the problems, I would have probably been too tired to find a solution. It hit me like a ton of bricks that I was now totally in charge of my family. I loved to run the show, but this was the most important show of my life. Was I ready?

Pete accepted a position in Alabama and the girls and I moved to Dublin, Ohio to be closer to Mom and Dad. They were my support system. Child support covered the babysitter, and I was compelled to find a real career to be the breadwinner and have the abundant lifestyle I desired.

I needed to be ready to hit the big time. I figured I was successful in small town radio, so onto big market Columbus radio. I could adjust from selling ads to strawberry farms to selling ads to huge car dealers, right? I set my intention for success, and trusted the Universe was listening. Once again, ready to jump into the pool ... would there be water in it this time?

The first thirty-something years of my life were a fun adventure, a pre-curser of what was to come. Change (transformation) was becoming my middle name ... from tomboy and animal lover to an independent and head-strong woman.

I thrived in the love and support of my parents, yet often needed to do things my way. My dad used to say, "Cathy listens to me, then goes and does what she pleases, but at least she listens."

What or who was I listening to? Was I starting to develop a relationship with my inner self, my inner guidance?

I may not have always been right, but I was never in doubt and steadily moving on to the next adventure.

The move to big city radio sales was the beginning of my biggest adventure yet ... and my formal introduction to spirituality. On to Columbus radio and meeting the two Patricias.

CHAPTER 2
My Journey, A.S. (After Spiritual)

"If you carry your childhood with you,
you never become older."
—Tom Stoppard

The stars were aligning ... I found a two-bedroom condo with full basement that I could almost afford in Dublin, only twenty minutes from Mom and Dad. The schools were top notch, in a safe neighborhood and the incentive to sell, sell, sell at my new radio station was prominent in my mind, so I could pay our rent.

Starting my new life as a single mom was ultra-exciting, which is just a flash thought away from being scared shitless. I knew I had to succeed, so onto playing with the big dogs and even fantasizing about getting back into the dating scene. In the next few months, I met two women who would have quite on impact in my life and both of their names were Patricia (one I called Patricia and the other Pat).

My big market Columbus radio station had an AM Talk Radio format and a FM Rock format. We could sell both. On the talk radio side, the morning show would periodically have a psychic (the first Patricia) as a guest. Patricia would answer questions from the listeners who would call in.

One day I was in the hallway outside the studio and Patricia was sitting on the couch, waiting to go on air. Patricia stared at me, then closed her eyes. Upon opening her eyes, in a gentle voice she said, "Just take a deep breath and relax, you will be fine. I know it's a big adjustment, don't worry so much ... this is just the beginning. You and your girls will all be fine." For one of the few times in my life, I was actually speechless. When I finally gained my composure, I stuttered, "How do you know that? How do you know we all will be fine?"

Patricia just smiled and shrugged her shoulders, "I just know ... that's what I heard." "Heard from who?" I tentatively asked. That started a discussion, a close friendship and my introduction to my internal spiritual side.

Every time Patricia came to the station, we had lunch together. I was reading every metaphysical book I could get my hands on, from Shirley MacLaine (*Out on a Limb* had just been released) to Richard Bach, Shakti Gawain (this was back in the 1980s) and especially Dick Sutphen. Patricia became my first spiritual coach and mentor.

I joined her and a group of five seekers in Sedona, Arizona for a Dick Sutphen retreat, including meditating in the Vortexes of the Red Rocks. I was hooked. I didn't totally understand everything yet, but I kept seeing my life being guided by these unseen spiritual forces.

Enter the second Patricia, the one I call Pat, a single mom of two teens. We met one night at a Parents Without Partners social mixer that we both thought was boring. All the guys there wanted to do was talk about how their ex-wives took everything. Pat suggested we check out another singles place, a bar we had both heard about in an upscale shopping center, called Sylvia's Back Door. So off we went ... adventure once again calling.

At Sylvia's we immediately found an abundance of guys to dance with, and as it turned out, to fight off come closing time. The last thing on their minds were their ex- or current wives. Having both been recently divorced, we were after excitement and out to prove our desirability, and the guys were there to assist.

What fun we had that summer. My daughters spent eight weeks with their Dad in Alabama, so I was ready and able to P-A-R-T-Y, something I had never really experienced, having married my high school sweetheart. But that fateful summer nearly did me in. Pat and I wrote a Bucket List of things we never had the guts to do and methodically started to check them off ... one crazy adventure at a time. I was experiencing huge doses of spiritual experiences as well as physical ones at the same time.

Pat and I would stay out till the wee hours at Sylvia's, and I would drag myself to the morning sales meeting at the radio station. I would tell my manager I was going to meet with new clients (I was going home and sleeping till late afternoon), check back in with the station, and off to Sylvia's to start the cycle again.

I was in another world—a world of sex, rock and roll, and alcohol ... lots of alcohol. It never dawned on me that you can't sell much radio advertising by sleeping the day away. So, by the end of the summer, I was thankful to see my girls come home. I was not so surprised to be out looking for another position.

No sales = No Commission = No job!

But what a summer! Pat and I packed a lot of living into those eight weeks. We continued to experience the singles scene but on a much less frenzied pace. We became life-long friends and still smile as we trip down memory lane, reliving our crazy, sexy summer. Thank you, Universe, for keeping me safe during my summer mis-adventures.

I was now in my late thirties and starting to realize I needed to find a real career, making real money, finding a pool filled with water this time. So, one evening a group of my friends invited me to a presentation about becoming a stockbroker. Of course, they made it sound so easy: play golf, schmooze, take clients to dinner, and make big bucks!

Sounded good to me! But it turned out to be selling "penny stocks" at Red Bird Securities. Okay, stop laughing ... it was another empty pool. But I did get my state securities license and realized that I was good at selling stocks. I just needed to relocate to a major wire-house brokerage firm. I set my intention, focused on my desire. and started to interview with the Columbus brokerage firms. I was really getting into this spiritual creating thing.

I was still working on the Trust and Allowing required to manifest my desires (I'll explain more about that later), and became impatient with the Universe's progress on the brokerage front. I continued to interview for other sales positions.

I answered an ad for a Toyota car salesperson and was hired on the spot. Not exactly what I had pictured, but the rent was coming due. Before speaking to each client that walked in the door, I set my intention to serve and honor them. It was long hours, but I enjoyed the selling interaction and practicing my new spiritual beliefs. I was starting to get the hang of selling cars and appreciated the Universe coming through for me once again when opportunity came a-knocking.

After only six weeks at Toyota, I was finally offered a stockbroker position. I was accepted as one of only a few women in the Dean Witter training class of 1987. It was decision time. I was feeling comfortable at Toyota, but my heart was in financial services. As you probably guessed, I said goodbye to selling cars and hello to selling stocks and bonds.

I started my illustrious fifteen-year career with Dean Witter (that has now morphed into Morgan Stanley) and was studying for the Series 7 exam when all hell broke loose. Three weeks after I joined Dean Witter, October 19, 1987 was Black Monday. The stock market crashed and fell almost 23 percent in one day. It was the largest percentage drop in one day ever! I thought, "Cathy, you are off to a great start!" Brokers were crying, many quit, and a few were even shot by their irate clients. This didn't go over well with Mom. Our office manager handed out T-Shirts saying "I survived the Crash of '87."

Yes, my entry into Dean Witter was quite an awakening. Going home that night, I was pretty shaken up and scared. What had I gotten into? This pool not only didn't have water, it was filled with snakes and alligators!

As I lay in bed that night, I closed my eyes and took several deep breaths, while asking for guidance. Now, what do I do? They are shooting brokers! After a few minutes, a peaceful, soothing feeling came over me and these wise words followed: "You don't even have clients yet—nobody is going to shoot you. The market is very low right now, that's the time to buy. With brokers quitting, who will work with these clients when the market comes back? ... And it will, as it always does. This is a good time to be getting in." I kept hearing myself reply, "Really? ... Really?" and a booming voice reply "REALLY."

Those feelings were right on, as I passed my Series 7, spent a month in New York City training in the World Trade Center and came back to settle in the downtown Columbus, Ohio Dean Witter office ... ready to make my fortune.

Well, the illusion of playing golf, schmoozing and client dinners soon faded into massive, massive cold calling. The water was starting to drain out of the pool, already. My manager gave me a sheet with numbers from 1-200 written on it, which represented the number of calls I was expected to make each day. I was instructed to put a "X" on the number if there was no answer, a diagonal line through the number if somebody answered and I got to give my pitch, circle the number if they were interested and add a star, if they bought something. Let me tell you, the "X" and "/" far outpaced the circles and stars.

The plan was a hundred calls before lunch and the remaining hundred in the afternoon. We did not leave for the night until all 200 dials had been completed. This was all before computers, although we did have an ancient version of a computer, called the Bunker Ramos to track the market gyrations.

It didn't take long to figure out, that I needed ten dials to speak to one person, and ten "warm bodies" would produce one interested, potential buyer.

Interested could mean, "Send me some information," or "Yeah, yeah, I'm interested ... now get off my phone," to really, actually interested. On a successful day, I would dig up two leads and pray they were really, interested. Without the benefit of computer leads, we purchased names on index cards. To keep my sanity and self worth in balance with all the rejection, I got revenge on those rude and inconsiderate people by tearing up their cards into little bitty pieces. Saying to myself, and sometimes out loud, "It's your loss baby, you don't get to work with me. Too bad for you!"

I quickly learned sales is a numbers game. The more people you talk to, the more people you sell. My job became known as "dialing for dollars." I spent many nights at the kitchen table, dialing my heart away, calling those people who did not answer during the day, while Andrea and Christine watched TV in the living room. During commercials, they would giggle and mimic me by singing "Hello, this is Cathy Brown, from Dean Witter. Do you like tax free income?" It wasn't easy, but the rent always got paid.

Soon magic happened. I started to get noticed in the office by increasing sales. The bigwig group, who thought it was fun to help the "cute, little newbie lady broker," suddenly realized I was out-producing them. The help stopped and the jealousy began.

I was increasing my sales, client list and income, but starting to get bored with the same ol' cold calling regimen. My focus was returning to where I was most comfortable: running the show.

Each night I visualized becoming some sort of a manager, training and coaching new brokers. I wanted to combine my teaching and selling skills to help others. I could feel a spiritual transformation from competitive selling to serving. This time, I just focused on the new direction and gave it up to the Universe.

It wasn't long till I was promoted to manager trainee and sent to New York City, back to the World Trade Center, to be a Manager Training Associate (M.T.A.), one of a team of six trainers, who taught the brand-new brokers from all over the United States, who had just passed their Series 7 exam. We received about 200 rookies every four weeks. We used to joke how we brought them in and churned them out. Once again, it was a numbers game, as the first year broker dropout rate was almost 40 percent.

I am still consistently amazed how you can create the life you want. Ask and you shall receive! The more I trusted in my creating partner, The Universe, the more my life was unfolding as I desired.

I loved teaching, consulting and coaching the newbie stockbrokers, which I did for six months before being sent to Pittsburgh to become the Office Sales Manager.

Another six months later, I was back in New York City, at the World Trade Center again, this time as Assistant Regional Director and elevated to Senior Vice President (S.V.P.).

This was in the mid 1990s, when many of the big investment firms were getting panned in the newspapers for being "Ol Boy's Clubs" and running rampant with sexual harassment lawsuits and for not promoting qualified women. We were merging with Morgan Stanley at the time, and as a P.R. move, they made a real effort to add women to senior management. I was riding the crest of that wave.

What a blast! Making big bucks, zipping around New York City in limos, traveling to beautiful resorts to run conferences and speak at awards meetings. It was not unusual to have seven or eight plane tickets at once, flying out each weekend. Once I got on a plane headed to Colorado, the only problem I was supposed to be going to Los Angeles.

Externally, it was an awesome adventure ... I was truly running with the big dogs. But, internally, I started to feel a yearning, that something was missing. It certainly wasn't the money, I was starting to lose my true, authentic self.

I had become a "closet" spiritualist. I never talked about my beliefs. I tried that once and pretty much got laughed at and ridiculed. The world of finance, which I had become a charter member of, was still that "Ol Boy's Club," and if I wanted to be included, it was best not to share my "Woo-Woo" beliefs. It was hard enough to be accepted as a woman, so I played along with their games. My external life was all that I thought success would bring, but my internal (96 percent spiritual) side took a beating.

Jerry and Ester Hicks, authors of many metaphysical best selling books such as *Ask and It Given,* talk about how important and powerful the spiritual component is within you. I was amazed to learn that only 4 percent of your thought and action process is physical. The remaining 96 percent comes from your inner guidance, your higher self, the Universe, your connection with God. When choosing to live your true authentic life, align first with the 96 percent, then engage your 4 percent physical actions.

Even though I was struggling with living authentically, I didn't gain much sympathy from my friends as I was pulling in nearly half a million a year. It was my first experience that money doesn't necessarily bring happiness, although it is a great perk. Not fully realizing it at the time, I was starting to feel this "living high on the hog lifestyle," as my Dad would always say, was short term, as I yearned for more meaning so that I could live my life with more authenticity, being more true to myself.

Things began to shift. Senior management changed and I was transferred to run the Tampa, Florida branch and a smaller satellite office in Winter Haven with nearly 200 brokers and support staff.

The transition was bumpy to say the least. Picture a hot shot, 5'2" petite blonde, New Yorker in super high heels, who walks and talks a mile a minute working with Florida's laid back version of that remaining "Ol Boy's Clubs". FUN, FUN, FUN! At least in New York, I always knew my detractors; they were right in your face, up front, no holds barred. They were so much easier to deal with than those guys dripping with honey and Southern charm, while stabbing you in the back.

As I became more focused on my spiritual growth, I had less of a desire to deal with their "gotchya" games. This all came to a head in September, 2001, when I had to return to New York City for a Branch Manager's meeting at the World Trade Center.

It started out to be one of the happiest weekends of my life as I flew from Tampa to Ohio for my daughter Christine's wedding. I was to fly from Ohio to New York City on Monday to attend the Manager's Meeting starting on Tuesday, September 11, at the New York University campus in mid-town.

The wedding was beautiful, not a dry eye in the church. However, as the weekend wore on, I started to get a sick feeling in the pit of my stomach. I was dreading returning to New York. This made no sense to me, as I would be going back to see all my old buddies. I was planning to have lunch with my former Regional Director of the New York Region and mentor on Tuesday afternoon at the World Trade Center. I had been looking forward to this reunion all summer. Looking back, I believe the Universe was preparing me for the horrific events of 9/11.

Tuesday morning was sunny with a clear blue sky so I decided to walk from my hotel to the meeting. Around 9 a.m., it happened. I looked up and saw an airliner fly directly into the twin towers. It was like the world stopped. I was frozen in time as I watched each floor of the towers in the World Trade Center complex systematically fall into a pile of ashes. People were screaming and jumping out of windows. It was unreal; like a scene from a disaster movie. Everything was quiet except for the rumble of the falling building and those screams, those horrific screams. The entire Universe seemed to be holding its breath.

Suddenly, large crowds of terrified people were frantically running towards me screaming and crying. In fear of being trampled, I pushed myself against a store's doorway as they ran past. Leaning against the store front, shaking and speechless, all I could think of were all those beautiful people that went to work this morning, just like me, not realizing they would not be coming home to their families tonight. I immediately grabbed my cell phone and called Mom and Dad to tell them I was alright, and to pass it on to the girls as I knew the cell phone lines were probably going to be jammed very soon. They had not yet heard about the attack and immediately turned on the news.

Then it flashed in my mind, it could have been me in those towers. Up until three months ago, my office was on the 68th floor of 2 World Trade. Why was I spared? Were my friends still alive? If the attack had been three hours later, I would have been in the towers having lunch with my mentor. Was he okay?

Nothing seemed to make sense. Nothing except sheer love for all those innocent people and gratitude that I was still alive. The next few days were sort of a blur. All the New York airports were shut down, and I was in charge of chaperoning a busload of panic stricken rookies traveling back to their Southern offices without any of their belongings, lucky to be alive.

It was a long, twenty-plus hour bus ride to return everyone to their families. When I finally arrived home, I noticed a letter taped to my front door from my next-door neighbor. It read, "I have been praying that you are alive." After being strong for all those young brokers on the bus, I just fell to the ground and wept on my doorstep. Thank you, Universe, for saving me. Life is too short. We don't know what tomorrow will bring. I then committed myself to living my life authentically and no longer wanted to hide my spiritual light under a bushel.

Once again, things started to move swiftly after that declaration. I had asked the Universe for assistance and, as always, it answered, but not exactly how I expected. About three months later, I was released (a nice way of saying ... fired) as manager of the Tampa Branch. I was called into the Regional Office one day (exactly one month after buying that $60,000 Lexus SC 460 Hardtop Convertible ... still trying to buy happiness and fulfillment), thinking I was to be congratulated for having a great month. I had raised our office production from seventh to third in the short time I had been there.

Instead of congratulating me, my regional director simply said, "Cathy, you are being released. Don't go back into the office again. You can come in after hours to collect your personal belongings. We will still pay you for a while, we may find another branch for you, but for now, you are done here."

My life was continuing to change, to transform. But, where to next? I had been moving (sprinting) up the corporate ladder in radio and financial services, well on my way to total material abundance.

I had it all ... job, house, car, money. I had it all, on the surface anyway. Why had this happened? Why was it all being taken away?

Was it being taken away or was I being set up for what I had been wanting all these years?

Yes, getting fired from what looked like a dream job was a bitter pill to swallow. I was soon to learn it was a real opportunity to learn about T.R.U.S.T: To Rely Upon Spirit Totally.

Ready to find out what happens next? Turn the page, please.

CHAPTER 3
Finally, on Track

"The only person you are destined to
become is the person you decide to be."
—*Ralph Waldo Emerson*

I felt like I had been whomped up the side of my head with a two by four. I had worked my ass off, put in long hours, above and beyond what was required, more than expected, and even survived the attack on the World Trade Center ... for what? To be fired by some small minded, two-bit, hot shot? To say the least, I was devastated. How unfair and unjust! But was it really?

Ever since my 9/11 declaration to live more authentically, more spiritually, I had wanted a change. But, did I want something this drastic? It seems that has been my history of working with the Universe. I set my intention, either consciously or unconsciously, and together we set up situations and opportunities to create those changes. If I miss the subtle opportunities presented, they become more and more prominent, more and more "in your face," so to speak.

It's hard to imagine something more prominent than 9/11, yet afterward, I was still at Morgan Stanley doing the work that was not really me. So ... the Universe needed to get my attention. This was not the last time I needed extra encouragement in the form of drastic measures, as you will see.

After the anger and total shock wore off, I realized maybe this wasn't so bad. I was receiving full salary (which lasted almost a year), living in sunny Florida, with a beautiful home and pool, with nothing to do but ... whatever I wanted to do. This would have been a perfect time to focus on me, meditate, connect with my inner self, and plan my next move.

Yes, it was the perfect opportunity ... but I opted to kick back, party some, travel some, work out at the gym some, study some and become a certified bartender—yes, you can get credentials in mixology. I threw fabulous parties and added a fully stocked bar in my living room with a mini version poolside. Man, could I make a mean Cosmo and an outrageous Mojito! But little time was invested on self-reflection and life planning.

One evening, the father of one of my close friends—who reminded me a great deal of my own father—sat me down and proceeded to read me the riot act. "Cathy," he said, "It's time to get off your butt and do something productive, something meaningful and worthwhile. You and my daughter are wasting time. You can't feel good about partying your lives away." I thought, really? I feel pretty good about not dealing with ANYTHING!

The next day, in the light of reason, I thought about what he said. He did have a point. The R & R was necessary, but not for the rest of my life. Enough was enough ... what was next?

My friend's father was a retired, licensed real estate broker, who was a silent partner of a small local firm. His daughter was also licensed in real estate and not happy in her current career. The plan was for me to get licensed, then we could both join his firm for experience, and later go out on our own.

Suddenly, I had a plan. Why not go into business with my best buddy and have her more experienced father watch over us? How hard can it be selling houses? I was good at selling stocks and bonds. Selling is selling, right?

As I was still receiving full pay from Morgan Stanley, and getting kind of bored with the leisurely lifestyle, I was off to jump into another pool. Would there be water or snakes and alligators in this one?

After a few months learning the business, I bought into a franchise and Weichert Realtors—1st Heritage was born. Another adventure was in the making. I discovered there was far more leeway in selling houses than investments. In the current housing market, they were selling like hotcakes. With the money pouring in, I felt fine when the Morgan Stanley checks stopped coming. Once again, the Universe provided for me ... it always had my back.

Even though all was going well, I still wasn't living my spiritual life to the extent I desired. I could be more open than at Morgan Stanley, but those twinges still haunted me. As the months wore on, those twinges got stronger. About a year later, the Florida real estate market tanked, the state was pummeled by hurricanes and sinkholes began to swallow up houses. Signs for me to move on were surfacing all over.

I was missing my family. Mom and Dad were getting up in years and both Andrea and Christine were married with children and living in Hilliard, Ohio. It was time to come home.

By now the Universe was probably getting disappointed with me because, once again, I did not take any time to really delve into what I was yearning for. I took a job as a Director of Career Services at a local college. It was fun for a while ... and it was great to be home with my family ... but it still was not my calling. About eight months in, there was a huge management shake-up and my new boss turned out NOT to be my biggest fan.

Ever had a job ... you hated? Well that was me. Any chance I found to stay home from work, I took. I think I'm getting a cold ... my leg hurts ... anything little thing at all. Subconsciously, I knew this job was toxic for me. It got so bad that I started to have back pain. I wound up walking like the hunchback of Notre Dame and was diagnosed with severe spondylosyndesis and needed back surgery.

You can tell how much I hated my job as I was almost looking forward to back surgery. The Universe was starting to get my attention now. The college granted me a twelve-week family and medical leave of absence. However, the first surgery was not successful and I needed a second operation. Since the college was only required to allow for twelve weeks of recovery, my leave was not extended and I was let go. I was actually relieved ... not a response you would imagine when losing your job. Next came the second back surgery, and another twelve weeks of recovery. I was on my back for three months, reading and watching Lifetime movies. I was now forced to take the time to focus on what I really wanted.

During the past twenty years I had not paid attention to the previous signs—being fired as a physical education teacher, Morgan Stanley corporate executive and college placement director. I had even survived the 9/11 tragedy. The Universe was consistently setting up opportunities for me to manifest my intention of living my true authentic spiritual life—but I was not listening. I was not yet ready.

During my three-month recovery from my second surgery, I finally took the time to just be still and finally listen to my inner guidance and what the Universe was setting up for me. I reflected on my life up to this point and began to understand the positives in each seemingly negative event.

Why did these events happen? I had created them to move forward in my spiritual transformation. When each opportunity presented itself, I froze, chickened out, was not ready. But now I felt the time had come. Something inside of me was changing, I was releasing my fear and increasing trust in myself and the Universe.

It's about that time, that I started getting emails from Christy Whitman, the founder of the Quantum Success Coaching Academy (www.christywhitman.com). I have no idea how she found me, I guess the Universe was working overtime.

The light finally came on. It was the turning point of my life. I signed up, completed my coaching certification and feel it was one of the best decisions of my life. Now, finally, I am living my true life, being my authentic self and living inside out.

It was a long journey to get here, but I wouldn't change a thing ... well, maybe a few incidents I don't fully remember. It would have been nice to catch on to the spiritual teachings earlier in my life, but I was not yet ready to accept them.

Many people might say, "Wow ... this chick was all over the place. What's her problem?" I was a Teacher, Gymnastics Coach, Radio Advertising and Car Salesperson, Stockbroker, Corporate Executive, Career Service Director and finally a Life Coach.

"She has lived in New Jersey, Ohio, New York, Pennsylvania, Germany, Florida and now back to Ohio. She can't seem stay put or stick with anything." They would be right. I am, and probably always will be, a seeker, looking for what is right for me. What is my calling?

Since you are reading this book, you are probably a seeker too. It makes no difference where you came from, your age or background. The important thing is where you are headed-because it is all about the journey.

Looking back, each seemingly unrelated career move, even the six-week stint selling Toyotas, was directing me to becoming closer to living the life I wanted. There seemed to be a common theme running through it all. All of my jobs centered around teaching, sales and coaching.

You see, selling in the most effective way, is providing clients with the information they need to make the decision that is best for them. We are all salespeople and coaches, sometimes selling others and always selling ourselves. Each decision we make is a sales closing. Done in a spiritual context, selling is coaching. Back in the day, they used to call it the "Consultant Sales Approach."

It may have taken me sixty-plus years to find my true calling (I hope you find yours sooner), but who cares? We are all here for the adventure, for the journey. You will get there when the time is right for you. Remember the old, but true adage, "When the student is ready, the teacher appears." If Christy Whitman had sent me those emails back when I was at Morgan Stanley, I probably would have hit delete. I wasn't ready yet.

Don't beat yourself up, if you are not there yet, for you are on your own journey, your own schedule. Your time will come if you intend it to. Since you are reading this now, you are well on your way, getting closer and closer ... and I am here to help.

My journey is far from complete. It is now my mission in life to help and guide others to discover their bliss and happiness by being a Law of Attraction Life Coach.

What exactly is a Life Coach? A professional Life Coach is a trusted mentor who can help you identify and uncover what is keeping you from reaching your fullest potential. We provide a support system while serving as an accountability partner, offering new perspectives, processes and techniques that you can use for the rest of your life. You will become self-reliant and self-empowered. You will be able to move forward with a greater momentum and clarity to realize your dreams.

A Law of Attraction Life Coach does all the above by using the spiritual principles, tools and techniques that I am excited to share with you in this book.

Let's journey on, seekers. The Universe and I have your back.

Ready for our first Foolproof Step to creating the life you want? Chapter 4 awaits.

CHAPTER 4
Foolproof Step #1: Clarity and Focus

"Clarity comes from knowing what you want and from moving in the direction of it. Your Soul is guiding you every step of the way."
—Sue Krebs

A while back, I was at the Humane Society, which is dangerous for me as it is hard not to bring a furry friend home as a playmate for Leo and Zen. I was watching a pile of cute little kittens playing. They were jumping, running this way and that, knocking into each other and even running around in circles. No direction, no rhyme or reason ... just running ... then after a while they just collapsed from exhaustion and fell asleep.

They were so cute and had quite an audience. I bet a few of them found a new family that day. As I was standing there, it got me to thinking ... how often do we just run around in circles without direction, until we drop from exhaustion? And ... we're not as cute as those kittens!

Do we know where we want to go, what we want our life to be? If you don't have clarity on where you want to go ... how do you know when you get there? Clarity is your GPS, your map to success.

Would you ever go to an airport, packed for a fabulous vacation, walk up to the ticket counter and say, "I want to buy a ticket?" Absolutely not, because the sales agent would look at you as if you're were dumb and say, "Where do you *want* to go?" I bet you always have a decent dose of clarity on planning your vacations. How about on planning your life? Before you can get the life, you want, you need to know *what you want!*

Seems simple, right? For many of us it's not simple at all. We are not living our own true, authentic selves, but rather living our lives for the expectations of others, or how we think we *should* be living our lives.

Let's stop here for a minute. I need to make a point and share with you one of the dirtiest words I know. No, not one of the ones that sometimes slip out when we are angry, but the one that is even more detrimental to us. That six-letter dirty word is *should*. This is a power stealing word. It means our true desires, thoughts and actions are taking a back seat to please others.

Have you ever wanted to pursue a career that your parents or loved ones disapproved of to choose another path more acceptable in their eyes, just to please them? That's a "should." You redirected your desire, in order to do something you thought you *should* do, maybe to keep peace.

That doesn't mean that you can never do something nice for another person. It only means for important, life choices, you come first. So, please add "should" to your list of unacceptable, dirty words.

Now that we have that out of the way ... let's continue. Some of us may be clueless as to what path to follow, while others feel they currently have too many goals or directions to pursue. That can be just as damaging. My Dad used to say "If you chase two rabbits, you're gonna lose both."

I remember when my daughters were young, Sears mailed an annual holiday toy catalogue. It was one of the most joyous events of the season when the "Sears Wish Book" arrived. Andrea and Christine, magic markers in hand, (Andrea—red, Christine—green) couldn't wait to carefully circle each toy they wanted for Christmas. There were very few uncircled pages in the entire 200 page "Wish Book."

I would then smile and say, "Santa doesn't have room in his sleigh for all those." Without missing a beat, they would reply, "Maybe Santa can make two trips." No ... No ... only one trip. We would then start to narrow down their choices to Top 25, Top 10, Top 5, and finally ... if you could have one and only one, which would it be?

This process repeated itself several times before mid-December, as the girls were easily influenced by the charismatic toy ads on TV. Just like we are sometimes distracted by the "shiny new object" in our life. Clarity is essential. What one thing do you want?

If you are struggling with no direction or too many directions and need to gain clarity, here are some revealing questions that will help. I discovered these on Facebook—yes, Facebook has more content than just cats playing the piano.

I strongly recommend you set aside some time to just relax and reflect upon these questions. Don't force yourself to come up with all the answers if they don't come immediately. Instead, just aim to explore the new ideas that come up or perhaps remember some you had forgotten about. Write down whatever ideas that pop into your head. You will be surprised to see where his exercise may lead you.

7 Essential Questions to Know What You Really Want to Do with Your Life

1. What did you dream about becoming when you were a child?
2. What would you regret not doing, being, or having in your life?
3. What activities make you lose track of time?
4. If you had to teach something, what would you teach?
5. What's your greatest accomplishment so far?
6. What does a perfect life look like to you?

7. What would you be doing if you had more money than you could spend?

How did it go? Were you able to find answers for all the above questions? Get some direction? Maybe you came up with several choices? Remember, Rome wasn't built in a day. Give it some time. Give it some thought. The answers will come.

Once you have a tentative direction, or several, it's time to dig deeper to decipher which may be the best action to take.

Here are three more short, but powerful questions, developed by my coach and mentor, Christy Whitman. Take each of your choices and ask yourself the following:

1. What do I want? (Insert your choice)
2. Why do I want it?
3. How will I feel when I have it?

This will narrow down your choices very quickly. The choice that makes you feel the best and whose why makes the most sense to you is your best selection. I wish I would have known these three questions back in the Sears Wish book days!

Now that you are clear on your choice, your goal, your action, add specifics so you can visualize it in every detail. The more specifically you can "see" your goal, the easier it is to focus on it and share it with your creating partner, the Universe.

The enemies of clarity are confusion and distraction. Once you have gained clarity and can visualize your desires, confusion doesn't stand a chance. When you can visualize in complete detail, there is no confusion.

Distraction may be another story. To beat distraction, we must develop our power of Focus.

Once you have clarity, you need to declare your intention (writing it down helps), and put your attention on that intention. That's kind of a tongue twister, isn't it? "Put your *attention,* on your *intention.*" In another words, focus on your clearly defined goal.

By focusing, I mean, put your energy and emotion into having that desire. Spend time focusing on that last question, "How will I feel when I have it?" Feel and focus on the essence of your goal.

Essence can be defined as the basic, real and intense nature, and indispensable quality. Spiritually, it is an inner knowing and emotional feeling. Behind every desire, is the longing to experience a certain feeling.

Let's say you want a cool, sports car, like I did with the Lexus hard top convertible back in my Morgan Stanley days. The essence of my dream car was the feeling I had when driving it. I could feel the wind blowing through my hair, the feeling of pushing down the accelerator on the freeway, heading to the beach, the scent of the salt sea air, the roar of the engine, the feeling like a million bucks, totally abundant, the freedom of the fun-loving lifestyle. This is feeling, the essence. I was really, really feeling it!

It's relatively easy to get this emotional high after you have acquired the object of your intention, but the key is to create those feelings *before* you physically have it!

Imagine or visualize you already have it. I know it sounds childish, but who has a more wondrous imagination than a child? Try it! Close your eyes, take a couple of deep breaths and start telling yourself a story about how you will be when you manifest what you want.

Remember those great stories we told as a kid? How creative we were, especially when we were trying to talk our way out of trouble. Mom, I didn't break that lamp, here's what happened ... Let's return to those days filled with wonder and imagination to visualize our new story, specifically how our life will be when our desire arrives. Feel the fulfillment and the inspiration.

Yes, it can and will arrive. How you ask?

Are you ready for the ride of your life?

Are you committed to create the life you want?

Let's Do It! First, we need a co-pilot. I am so excited to introduce you to the Universe, your co-creating partner and one of its assistants, The Law of Attraction.

Oops! We are getting a little ahead of ourselves. Before we get the introductions going and head off to create, we need to spend a moment with the concept of energy. John Assaraf, best-selling author, explained that Nobel Prize-winning physicists have proven the physical world is one large sea of energy flashing in and out in milliseconds, over and over again. Nothing is solid. This is the concept of Quantum Physics.

Everything in the world is energy, and energy emits a vibration. You, me, our pets, even the chairs we sit on ... everything in the Universe is energy, and we all send out a vibration.

Our thoughts are linked to this invisible energy, sending out the vibration, determining what the energy forms. Your thoughts shift the Universe to create your life. That's incredibly powerful, isn't it?

Here's how it works. Your thoughts create the vibrations that work like little magnets going out into the Universe attracting similar vibrations. You have probably heard the saying, "Like Attracts Like." Best-selling Author, Mike Dooley, always tells us, "Thoughts become things, choose them wisely."

First, get clarity on what you want. Be as specific as you can—adding all the details and especially the feelings and emotions. Then, focus with laser precision on those feelings and visualizations—the essence—a if you already have what you desire.

This is where the Law of Attraction comes into play. You attract what you are focusing on ... your thoughts become the energy vibrations that you send out into the Universe searching for other like vibrations.

But what if you send out negative thoughts? Let's get more involved with Foolproof Step #2, The Law of Attraction.

CHAPTER 5
Foolproof Step #2:
The Law of Attraction

"We become what we think about.
Energy flows where attention goes."
—Rhonda Byrne

We can all now agree: we attract what we are focusing on. Good attracts good and unfortunately, bad attracts bad. What we send out, vibrationally, always comes back to us. That's because the Law of Attraction is impartial and non-judgmental, always saying "yes" to whatever you are focusing on. It does not distinguish if you are sending out thoughts about what you want or what you don't want—it always sends back a match. That's the law. It's the Quantum Physics.

Just like the Law of Gravity, if you drop a ball out of a window, it always falls downward, never sideways or up. That's also the law. If you are focusing on all those bills you can't pay ... what are ya gonna get? Bingo ... more bills you can't pay.

I learned about the negative manifesting the hard way. A few years back I was driving home from a visit with my mom, who was ninety-six at the time and living in an assisted living facility as my dad has transitioned a year earlier at age ninety-four. (I've got good genes, thank you Universe). The visit didn't go too well. She was not in the greatest mood. At ninety-six, Mom's demeanor was often unpredictable.

I was not in the greatest mood either as I was driving home. I was feeling a little sorry for myself, wondering why Mom couldn't be happy to see me, as I was so busy, yet I was taking time to spend with her when I could be doing so many other, in my mind, more productive activities. I was far from accepting of her feelings, aches and pains. I now realize it would have taken so little to be more understanding. What type of energy do you think I was sending out?

About half way home, a large SUV, in the middle lane, suddenly decided to make a right turn. Too bad I was in the right lane! I slammed on my brakes just as I saw her cut in front of me, but couldn't stop quick enough to avoid her smashing into my left side. At least by hitting my brakes, I avoided a much worse collision. I went ballistic.

We pulled over and the negative energy was swirling as she spoke only in broken English, couldn't find her license, and was driving her brother's car. I could feel the anger flaring up inside of me. This was my first accident in over twenty years.

I didn't think to call the police, just my insurance company. My agent tried unsuccessfully to understand the other driver. Getting nowhere, my agent suggested to just stop the confrontation and take my car in for an estimate. She booked an immediate appointment.

I was still furious as I drove to the dealer for a damage estimate.

Why did this happen to me?

I was not taking responsibility for creating the events in my life at all. Cooling my heels in the dealer's waiting room, helped a little, but you could still cut through my negativity with a knife.

The mechanic kept coming in and saying, "Relax, it will be fine," but I wasn't buying it. The estimate came to about $1,200, of which $500 was my deductible. This just increased my anger and negativity. I didn't stop to think that if I was not at fault, I would be totally covered, nothing out of pocket.

I begrudgingly thanked the mechanic, got back into my car and backed out of the service bay ... right into a brand-new car. That's right ... I ran into another car. The second accident that day! This time there was no question who was to blame ... only myself. Remember how I mentioned that sometimes the Universe has to whomp me up the side of my head before I get it? Once again, lesson learned, the hard way.

The negativity from Mom's visit affected my little vibrational magnets going out in the Universe searching for like vibrations. Negativity = Negativity, for me, not only once, but twice!

A word to the wise ... Be open to your feelings and thoughts. We all have negative emotions from time to time. Don't wait to act. Pivot, or turn your focus to a better feeling thought as soon as you can. It's like walking into quicksand. Get out as soon as you notice that sinking feeling. If you wait too long, you will be up to your neck in quicksand, or in my case, up to two accidents in one day.

Now whenever I start to go negative, I take a step back, take a few deep breaths, and focus on something positive. I call it going to my happy place. I flash back to a fun family vacation to Punta Cana, Dominican Republic a few years ago. My entire family was enjoying the sunshine and beach. The kids were playing in the sand and surf and the adults were basking in the sunshine with margaritas nearby. Not a care in the world. Everyone was happy, rested and carefree. Every time I think of that scene, I automatically smile. That's my happy place.

Find your "happy place" and keep it ready to go to whenever you start to feel negativity knocking. That's called pivoting. By focusing your thoughts and attention on a subject for only a few seconds, you begin a vibration of that thought within you. The Law of Attraction answers that focus. The longer you keep your thought on that subject, the easier it is to keep focusing on it because you are attracting more thoughts and vibrations like those original thoughts. You begin to feel the essence, the good feelings, the true nature of your initial thought. Remember, The Law of Attraction means like attracts like.

From the teachings of Abraham-Hicks, we learn that it takes a mere seventeen seconds to start to activate a new focus, gain clarity and have it become strong enough for the Law of Attraction to begin to bring matching vibrations. At this point, the vibration does not have much attracting power, but by continuing to focus, the power quickly increases. Within sixty-eight seconds of pure focus, the intended vibration is powerful enough to begin its manifestation. Focusing on the positive is much better than having two accidents in one day. Lesson learned!

We create from the inside. Our outer (physical) world is simply mirroring back to us what is going on in our inside (spiritual, energetic) world. I remember a song I love by Garth Brooks called, "The Dance." It reminds me that we are living our own dance between the spiritual (inner) and the material (outer) world.

I can't hit on this point enough. Your inner world controls your outer reality. You are totally responsible for your life, no more blaming others. It took me two accidents in one day to learn that one. So, if you are not happy with your physical life, what do you do? You change your inner thoughts and vibrations.

This works ... it really works. I have a much more positive story to share with you now. This one is about the positive vibrations.

In 2014, I enrolled in Christy Whitman's Quantum Success Coaching Academy (QSCA) program, totally focused on becoming a great Law of Attraction Life Coach. I was about halfway through the program when I heard about the annual QSCA Business meeting in California. Invitations were sent to all graduates and students to gather for the weekend to network, learn from noted metaphysical speakers while meeting the instructors and Christy herself.

This sounded like something right up my alley. I hadn't had a proper vacation in a few years and the opportunity to meet Christy was just too much to resist. I signed up on the spot.

On the flight from Ohio to California I was reading *The Prosperous Coach*, by Steve Chandler and Rich Litvin. The authors made a point about how you can only take a client as far as you are willing to go yourself. How can you expect a client to buy into the concept of coaching if you don't buy into it enough to have a coach yourself and continue to grow in your business and personal life? That was an Aha! moment for me.

As a real newbie to coaching, I was excited about starting a new career but concerned about having so little knowledge in building a website, online marketing and getting clients. I wanted and needed a coach to assist me in getting my new coaching practice off to a successful start.

As I sat there, somewhere 30,000 feet over Colorado or Utah, I set my intention. I am going to get a coach this weekend. I had no idea who, or how, but I was getting my coach this weekend. I closed my eyes and asked the Universe to assist in bringing my coach to me. Then I let to go of my intention. Every time I thought about the upcoming meeting, I felt the essence of my new coach.

The flight was great, the hotel in San Diego was fabulous and the meeting was inspiring. I met so many spiritual minded people and developed many lasting friendships. I sat in the front row for all the sessions as my 5'2" stature made it difficult to see over people sitting in front of me. I had almost forgotten about my intention of finding my coach with all the activities and excitement of the speakers and seeing Christy Whitman live.

Then on Saturday, just before lunch, it happened. Christy began to explain a new mentoring program she was starting. It was not for everybody, only a select group of five to six coaches who wanted to excel in their business. I nearly fell off my chair. THAT WAS IT! Christy was going to be my coach. I just had to do this. It never crossed my mind that I was only six months into the training, that there were over one hundred people in the audience, many more qualified than me. I just knew Christy was going to be my coach. Talk about feeling the essence! I came back to reality to hear Christy say she would give all the details after lunch.

As she finished and released us all for our lunch break, I jumped up and ran to the stage where Christy was collecting her notes. It felt as if I was running on pure adrenalin as I stammered quite loudly, "Christy ... I'm a ... I'm Cathy Brown, and I want to do this ... I really want this." I must have sounded like a crazy person, a bit off balance. I felt the Universe was setting this up for me.

Christy turned around, smiling, sort of giggling, I think, and said "Okay Cathy, I'll get the application to you after lunch." I was on cloud nine. I wanted a coach, but I never thought it would be Christy Whitman. Christy was a New York Times bestselling author, and CEO and founder of the QSCA. WOW! Once again, I didn't give any energy to the fact that I was probably one of many applying for the mentorship, and one of the least qualified.

That afternoon, along with many others, I filled out the application and just let it go. I allowed the Universe to take control trusting that the result would be in my best interest. (More on allowing and trusting coming soon.)

Little did I know; Christy was intrigued with me. She was genuinely impressed that I was willing to commit and trust the Universe to bring this to me without having any of the details, investment or anything. I appeared to have total trust in her and in the Universe. Once again, I was ready to jump into that pool. Was that pool ready for me?

Unknown to me at the time, Christy started to "check me out" by talking to my instructor and others who knew me from the program. The Universe was setting things in motion. During the final session on Sunday, Christy thanked all of us who applied, saying she would email those selected early next week.

My homeward-bound flight was scheduled on Monday morning. While waiting in the lobby for the airport taxi, I heard somebody calling my name. I turned around to see Christy walking over to me, smiling. She gave me a big hug, whispering, "Congratulations, you are in the mentor program. I'm going to be your coach."

This is one of the other times I couldn't speak. When I finally realized I was in ... all I could say was "It works, this stuff really works," then of course, "Thank you so much!" Christy looked as bit puzzled and replied, "Great, yes it does work."

The Law of Attraction is always working, carrying your waves of energy and vibrations out to the Universe. Once you truly feel the essence of what you want to bring into your life, allow and trust in the power of the Universe to create it. People and opportunities will start to flow into your life to assist you in achieving your goals. A certain synchronicity begins to bring in all you need. You are now Deliberately Creating.

The Law of Attraction, "Like Attracts Like," means your thoughts become your vibrations. Your vibrations flow out into the Universe to connect and match other like vibrations.

The Universe doesn't distinguish between positive and negative thoughts and vibrations. It just sends back a match to whatever you are sending out.

It's up to you. Do you want to create two accidents in one day, or a wonderful coach? It is your choice. This brings us to the Law of Deliberate Creation.

CHAPTER 6
Foolproof Step #2, Continued:
The Laws of Deliberate Creation and Allowing

"Nothing can occur in your life experience without your intention of it through your thoughts."
—Abraham-Hicks

The Law of Deliberate Creation is a cool law, because this law gives us the power to choose our own thoughts. The Law of Attraction is working non-stop, whatever vibrations you send out will come back, good or bad. You have the choice: to create by deliberately choosing your thoughts, or create by default. Do you want to be in control or not? Either way, what you send out comes back. Be in charge or take what you get?

There is no judgment on what you create (or just let happen), but there are consequences that follow your thoughts or intentions. Those consequences are the experiences we call our life.

If you are not happy with your life right now, or desire more happiness, it's all in your hands. In the words of Dolly Parton, "If you don't like the road you are walking on ... start paving another." Change your thoughts, change your life. It's all about the those "Good Vibrations," remember that Beach Boys song?

How do you know what thoughts or vibrations you are sending out? Simple answer ... how do you feel? Pay attention to how you feel emotionally. Take a gut check periodically during the day. If you feel anxious, worried, angry or depressed, I bet you are focusing on the negative stuff, or something you don't want. That's okay for a short time, because it brings clarity to what you do want. If you know what you don't want (contrast), it's easier to know the opposite, what you do want (clarity).

Here's what I mean. I have a nervous stomach when I think about failing an upcoming exam. I know I don't want to fail that test. What do I want? I want to pass that test. I change my focus to seeing and feeling the success of a passing grade, maybe even acing it. First I switch the vibration (pivot), then I take action to prepare and study to get that good grade I am visualizing. Then, just before I am scheduled to take the exam, I set my intention, get connected with myself and the Universe, and ask for help and support (alignment). Then I start the exam (momentum). I will explain more completely about alignment-momentum in a Chapter 9.

Abraham-Hicks shares the three Steps to Creating and Manifesting:

1. You ASK
2. The Universe ANSWERS
3. You RECEIVE

In Step 1 "You Ask," is Deliberating Creating, choosing what you want.

Step 2 brings in the Law of Attraction, matching what you are asking for, and focusing on what you want, not what you don't want.

Step 3, receiving is a bit more difficult than most of us realize. This is the Law of Allowing, which could also be called the "Law of Accepting."

Before you can change something, you must first accept conditions as they are. If you hate your job and want to find another, those negative vibrations leak into your creating, and you may find another job with the same challenges.

Before you ask for a new job, find something to appreciate in your current position. It may be insignificant, but needs to be something positive. Maybe you like the people you work with, the cafeteria has good and economical food, or the parking lot is close to the building so it's a short walk on cold or rainy days. Anything to replace the negative with some positive. That's acceptance.

You are accepting the situation, but at the same time, you would like to improve it. Accept what is, now change to what you would like. I have a sign in my office that reads, "It is what it is, but it will become what you make it."

I did not do that with my job as Director of Career Services. I just hated it ... negative, negative, negative ... and the result was two back surgeries. During my tenure there, I interviewed for several other positions, but was not hired for any of them even though I was highly qualified. Wonder why? Lack of acceptance. Accept what is—create what you want!

Christy Whitman shared with me the three Relationships involved with Allowing:

1. With Yourself
2. With Others
3. With the Universe

First accept yourself, not after you lose those fifteen pounds or find the love of your life, accept yourself now.

Who are you deep down?

Is that the same or different to how you appear to others in the outside world?

Are there things you need to change to truly love and accept yourself and be happy in your own skin?

Love and accept yourself just as you are now, warts and all. You are unique. There is nobody else on earth exactly like you. You're pretty special, don't you think?

The second aspect of Allowing is your relationship with others. This is a big one, because many of us seem to give away our power to others. If your happiness depends upon your boyfriend or girlfriend, husband or wife, etc., changing somehow—by making more money, treating you better, even to stop wearing those ugly, smelly sweat pants—you are relying on others to control your happiness. You are living outside-in, rather than inside-out.

You are totally responsible for your own life and happiness. The fact that your boyfriend lives in sweats is not your problem, unless you allow it to be. Your decision is to accept it (with positive feelings) or move in another direction. His choice of wardrobe does not have the power to negatively impact your life, unless you allow it to. Then, shame on you. That's when you are giving away your power.

You may accept somebody as they are. That doesn't mean you must agree with them. You are simply allowing them to be who they are, without having it bother you. When you are not accepting, you are resisting. You can't receive when you resist.

Meredith Savers, yoga instructor, has written, "The most important part of any relationship is allowing others to choose their own response, and of course this is the most difficult part." I totally agree with Meredith, allowing IS challenging.

In 1987, I became a single parent. After fifteen years of marriage, I found myself divorced with two young daughters to care for. If I had second-guessed myself, by thinking I should (there's that dirty word I told you about) have stayed married, I would have brought up all those negative emotions. Those are the resistance emotions like fear, doubt and anger. With all that fighting against what is and those angry and frustrated feelings toward my ex (so much resistance), how could I show up as a loving mother for my girls?

Once again, it took time, it did not happen overnight, but I got it. I could accept my "now" situation, and find appreciation in my two beautiful daughters who gave me strength and compassion. Once I accepted and allowed my situation, my heart opened, I settled down and started to build my life to be how I wanted it to be. And even though it took a little longer, I allowed my ex to do the same.

True empowerment comes from being able to let go of the people and situations that are toxic for you while harboring no ill will toward them. You will then allow in more support, love and appreciation from those around you.

Allowing, for me at least, seems to be a life-long pursuit. I thought I had it mastered, experiencing being dismissed from gymnastics coaching and surviving divorce until once again, it reared its ugly head. In 2001, back in my

Morgan Stanley days, I had been transferred from the New York region to sunny Florida to run a branch in Tampa. I was there about six months, bought a house and thought I had made the transition from the fast-paced New York City to leisurely Florida—and thought all was well. I had raised the office revenues, hired successful stockbrokers, and even brought my Lexus hard-top convertible. Life was good ... no, life was great!

Suddenly, out of the blue (or so I thought) I got fired. Seems that the regional management changed and the new guy in charge wanted to put his buddy in my job. I was devastated. It took me some time to realize how to benefit from the Law of Allowing.

If I kept being against the firing, being in resistance, focusing on why this happened to me or what I could have done differently, that's not being in the place of allowing and acceptance.

The important key here ... You must be in a place of accepting to move forward. It doesn't happen overnight, and you don't have to agree or approve of everything, but only once you learn to accept it can you move on with your life.

If you stay devastated, angry, and depressed, who are you hurting? Right, yourself. If that firing had not happened, I probably wouldn't have become a life coach and wouldn't be sharing here with you today. It was really for my benefit.

I traveled that Allowing journey again with my mom, who in 2014, entered hospice at age ninety-seven. Mom had been doing great for so many years, surviving my dad who transitioned in 2013 at age ninety-five. Recently, heart problems, refusal to eat or drink, along with respiratory problems had put her into the hospital three times in two weeks with no improvement. Now was the time to love and allow Mom to take her journey home.

In allowing my mom the freedom and support for that journey, I learned the true meaning of allowing, accepting and unconditional love. It was hard for me to not try to fix the situation, choosing instead to accept "what is."

Sitting with my mom, talking some, but mainly just watching her sleep brought back so many wonderful memories that I had not thought about in years. The times we spent walking to the bus, Mom's leadership of my Brownie and Girl Scout troops, spending overnights at my house when my girls were little, her unconditional love and support. Mom has always been my greatest cheerleader!

Now I had the opportunity to be her greatest cheerleader and allow her to be with Dad in love and light. I helped her complete her journey, by not resisting, but by allowing her to do it her way.

Imagine growing in complete acceptance of yourself and all those around you, adding the love and support and living the life you desire. These are the experiences you will attract when you focus on Allowing.

I confess, I struggled with accepting and allowing. I still work on it. You could say I am a work in progress, but it is getting easier because I have experienced so many wonderful results.

It's never easy, especially if you are a strong, independent, "in charge and loves to run the show" kind of person. It takes a lot of practice, but it is well worth the effort. First allow—then receive. We can only receive as much as we are willing to allow and accept.

We now know that we have the power, as well as the total responsibility for creating our lives. It is up to us. We choose our thoughts and vibrations, we deliberately create the world we live in, while allowing others to do the same.

Their actions and behaviors do not affect us, unless we allow them to affect us. It's always our choice. Allowing and accepting ourselves and others is the way to build loving, lasting and abundant relationships.

We also have another very important relationship to build, our relationship with the Universe. This is the relationship totally based on Trust. This is the biggie! Are you ready to tackle it now? Let's get started.

CHAPTER 7
Foolproof Step #3: Trust

"Allowing and trust are the same thing."
—Abraham

The first two parts of Allowing are your relationships with yourself and others. The final part of Allowing is your relationship with the Universe. I keep talking about the Universe. What exactly is the Universe? It can be many different things to many different people. Some think it is God, others feel it's our greater power, our spiritual guidance, inner strength or total creative energy

For me, the Universe is my higher power, my loving and supportive creative partner, who is always looking after my best interest. It is my unseen, but highly felt, all knowing and all supporting (almost fairy godmother-like) energy. It's there, just waiting to be of assistance in delivering what I ask of it. I feel secure in that it always has my back. I ask—It answers.

Your relationship with the Universe is precious, one of the most precious and enduring relationships of your life. This relationship is created entirely on TRUST! Through my certification with the Quantum Success Coaching Academy, I learned T.R.U.S.T. means ...

To

Rely

Upon

Spirit

Totally

Sanaya Roman and Duane Packer in the book Creating Money, published by H J Kramer and New World Library, 2008,(www.orindaben.com), define Trust as "The opening of the heart, believing in yourself and in the abundance of the Universe. It is knowing that the Universe is loving and friendly and supports your higher good. Trust is knowing that you are a part of the process of creating and believing in your ability to draw to you what you want."

What's the difference between trust and hope? Trust is believing and knowing what you asked for will come, while hope is wanting something without truly believing it will arrive.

I trust in my partnership with the Universe. I hope I will be President someday. See the difference? One I know and believe, the other not so much.

I once had a client who I introduced to the Law of Attraction. He couldn't wait to try it out. I suggested he decide on something he wanted, focus on it, believing it would come and report on the results the following week.

At next week's session, he showed up disappointed, complaining that the Law of Attraction stuff was a crock. It didn't work. It was all fake. I quickly jumped in, asking him what he had asked for ... he responded smugly, "To win the 3-million-dollar jackpot lottery on Saturday night." Kind of a big ask for the first time, don't you think?

I then asked him, "Did you truly believe and know you would win that?" He laughed, "No ... not a chance in hell could I win that!" Do you see the disconnect here? He may have been hoping, but he was certainly not trusting.

The key is to build trust while you build your skills with the Law of Attraction and your relationship with the Universe. I suggest you start with something small, something you truly believe you can have. I began with a good parking space at the mall.

Every time I went shopping, I set my intention to find a parking spot close to the stores I planned to visit. Driving in, I set my intention, focused only on the preferred parking area and truly believed with my inner knowing I would find it. And it happened! Woo hoo!

Now, that may not seem like such a huge accomplishment to you, but my trust grew. It worked ... it really worked! By acting, intending to find the perfect parking space, I put my trust into action. I took a risk—no matter how small at first—and increased my ability to trust and believe in myself. The smaller the risk you take at first, the less resistance, or negative disbelief you will have.

By developing trust, you put your intention into action, get feedback and see results. This demonstrates to the Universe that you truly intend to have what you desire. It shows you are ready, trusting and able to create. All systems go!

The more confidence you gain, the larger your intentions can become. I was in total trust when I set my intention to have Christy Whitman as my coach. It is reasonable to set your intention on winning that lottery with total belief and trust. However, I suggest you work up to that, by starting with the parking space-type intentions first.

I have been talking about my silver Lexus sports car in previous chapters, but I haven't told you how it all came about. Trust was an integral part of its coming to life. I fell in love with that car when I was in New York City working for Morgan Stanley. My regional director had purchased one a few months previously, and as soon as I saw it, I was in love with it ... maybe obsessed is a better description.

I thought about that car all the time. I went to the New York City Annual Car Show, took photos of the car, and brought a brochure home. I put a color photo of the exact car I wanted up on my desk, silver with black interior. I could even feel how it would be to drive it. I felt the essence. I went to the dealership, took a test drive. It was brand new ... so I had to order it, six months waiting list. I was living in New York City at the time and there was no way I could pay the $60,000 price tag, plus it probably was not smart to have a convertible and drive it into the city each day. I usually took the train.

However, by the time it arrived, I had moved to Florida, having been promoted to manage my own office. My new salary and bonus could easily afford the $1,000 monthly lease payment. I did not know of the move and promotion when I desired that car, but I just knew that somehow, I would have it. The Universe put into motion all that needed to take place to bring that car to me.

Trust is the link between the mental world and the physical world. It provides continuity during the time lapse, or gap, between the inner belief and when it manifests in the physical world. Once you set your intention, your dreams are already real in the mental plane; they are just waiting for the perfect time to appear in your physical world. Trust your higher self to bring you the right things at the right time. Sunny Florida was ideal for a convertible. It was the perfect car for the sunshine state. Way to go, Universe!

Generally, things don't happen immediately (except maybe parking spaces, the little stuff). I had to get a promotion and move to Florida before I got my car. There is usually a lag time, a gap, while the Universe is setting things in motion.

As a rule of thumb, the larger or more complicated an intention, the more time it may take. That's why trust is so important. Trust keeps your thoughts and vibrations high (out of the negative quicksand) while you are waiting. The more positively focused and trusting you are, the quicker your desires manifest.

Timing is also very important. If my Lexus had arrived while I was still in New York City, I wouldn't have been able to drive it that much, let alone pay for it (monthly garage rentals in the city were more than apartments in the Midwest). The six month wait list gave the Universe plenty of time to set things in motion, first by creating the promotion and move to Florida, then bringing in the car. You need to keep those vibrations high during that waiting period, knowing and believing it will come. Trusting, not hoping, it will come. The Universe brings your desires at the best time for you. This may not always be on *your* timetable, but the all-knowing, all supportive Universe's timetable. That's the time when you may receive the most benefit from having it.

This is where the Law of Detachment enters the picture. Detachment is the giving up control of the details of your manifestation; the *how* and *when*. In another words, totally focus on your intention, feel the essence and vibrations, keeping your eye on the prize, but detach from the results. Give control of the how and when to the Universe.

Feelings of control and attachment to the result come from fear, lack, insecurity or lack of trust. In detachment, you have the freedom to create. It is totally freeing to allow the Universe to take the wheel and drive the creating process. Your part is to positively focus, feel the essence, while the Universe's part is to bring it forth at the best time, for your best benefit. Don't step on the Universe's toes. Both of you do your part in creating. It works best that way.

Here's a personal example of the Law of Detachment in action. I was living in Florida in 2005, selling my real estate company, wanting to come back to Ohio as my entire family was there. I had been away too long. I put my house on the market, and acted as my own realtor. I had planned to stay in Florida until my house sold. I held open houses, broker special tours, everything I could think of to sell the house quickly. You could say I was very attached to the outcome! I tried to control the outcome. I was based in fear and insecurity—I was not detached at all.

I was totally attached to the outcome because one of my daughters was pregnant with her second child and I wanted to be in Ohio for her. I decided to turn the selling of my house over to the Universe—no strings attached—now I was finally detached!

On the next trip to Ohio, I found a home to purchase and started the ball rolling—only focusing on the intention to sell, and going about my business. I was planning to move in sixty days, regardless if the Florida house sold or not. I released the outcome to the Universe and stayed attached only to the intention—to sell the house—not the how or when.

Magically, as soon as I decided to move ahead with my plans to move to Ohio—to purchase the Ohio house—and to set my departure date, within a week, I had an outstanding offer with a $100,000 profit margin. We closed the day before I had scheduled to leave for Ohio. Moral of the story ... detach and allow your desires to come to you.

It's all about TRUST. The Universe was setting up all the events for me to sell my house. Remember the meaning of **TRUST: To Rely Upon Spirit Totally.**

When you know that Spirit will give you what you need—not necessarily what you think you want—then you will learn to do the work that is required to be done and move on. The results will take care of themselves. The timing of how things manifest will come at the perfect time. When we trust, the Universe knows what the perfect timing is and it happens even faster because we get out of the way.

In the words of French philosopher and mystic, Simone Weil, "Attachment is a manufacturer of illusion and whoever wants reality ought to be detached."

Please allow me to share one more life story about trust and detachment. It is a deeply personal one (you may want to get a Kleenex). I previously mentioned that my Dad transitioned in 2013 and Mom followed in 2014. Their wish was to have their ashes spread together wherever the family chose.

We all racked our brains and finally picked The Park of Roses as Mom had always loved roses, receiving them for every birthday and anniversary. In fact, one of her friends nicked named her "Rosie."

We waited for the roses to be in bloom and scheduled the entire family outing to be followed by a celebration of life dinner at a steakhouse (as my Dad loved steak—medium rare).

As the now matriarch of the family, I felt a responsibility to plan the event and a little service after the spreading of the ashes. If you know me, preparation is my middle name. If I am to make a presentation, no matter how short—I practice, practice, practice. But this time I could not write my little talk ... something wasn't working, I seemed to be forcing it.

As I thought about my writing block, I heard the words, "STOP ... Don't prepare. TRUST and speak from your heart, the words will come." It took all my strength to **not** prepare and just ALLOW the Universe to bring me the exact words I needed at the exact right time.

Soon the day came—and it was pouring rain all day. I kept thinking ... do we cancel? Reschedule? Once again, I heard,

"STOP, remember to TRUST—Just ask and it is given." So, at noon, I set my intention: "Rain stops from 5:00 p.m. to 7:00 p.m."

As soon as I set my intention, I felt better. The rain kept falling all day as we drove to the Park of Roses, the umbrellas in the trunk. I told you I am still a work in progress.

We parked the cars and started walking toward the park—about five minutes into the park (umbrellas up) we passed a pretty gazebo and a line of roses bushes in full bloom that just felt right. We all agreed this was the place. Guess what happened? The rain stopped! I just smiled—shook my head and raised my eyes to the heavens and said "Thank You." Guess what time it was? I still get chills when I remember that day.

As I was opening the containers to spread the ashes, I was concerned how the little ones (two family members were four years old) would react. I didn't want them to be afraid or feel uncomfortable. Just as that thought came to mind, one of my daughters spoke to the two little ones saying, "MaMa and BaBa have helped us all so much to grow and prosper—now they can help the roses to grow." Perfect timing ... and a wonderful sentiment. It felt so loving and natural. We all took turns lovingly giving Mom and Dad to the roses.

I'll never forget my youngest four-year-old little grandson, taking his father's hand and walking all the way down to the end of the row where a small rose bush was struggling to grow. He looked up at his dad and said, "Daddy, this bush is so little, it needs some MaMa" as he so very gently spread Mom's ashes around the roots. Such a wonderful tribute from the lips of a four-year-old.

After spreading the ashes, we walked back to the gazebo. Standing in a circle, holding hands, I closed my eyes and allowed the Universe to speak through me. I honestly can't tell you what I said ... only that my family all hugged me saying, "Mom that was wonderful." We then played a CD called "There Is Only Love" by Karen Drucker.

The rain stopped, my talk was moving and the ceremony was loving and meaningful. I believe it was all because I trusted the Universe to come through for me; I got out of the way (detaching) and allowed my desires to come forth. It was my confirmation that the Universe is a loving and friendly place where desires are fulfilled if you allow, trust, detach and show gratitude.

> *"Breathe, the Universe is taking care of everything else." —Astrology.com*

To assist you in working on your trusting, here is as fun exercise from Sanaya Roman and Duane Packer's wonderful book, *Creating Money—Attracting Abundance.*

Trusting

1. List as many items as you can that you wanted, imagined or fantasized about having and then received.

2. For several of the items you listed, recall the level of trust you had that you would get them. Describe how this trust felt, how you felt as you waited for these things to come, or what you did that affirmed your trust that they would come.

3. List as many items as you can that you want now. Which do you trust that you will create?

4. Pick one from your list. What action could you take to demonstrate that you trust you will get it?

What did you come up with?

Get some ideas? Here's a thought, write your answers and come back in a few months to see if they have changed or evolved.

I feel you are well on your way to developing your powers of deliberating creating, allowing, trusting, and detaching.

We have talked about accepting your current situation while you are creating a better one. Now let's take acceptance a little further. Let's increase acceptance by adding appreciation!

Each night before I go to sleep, I give thanks for my day. I even appreciate my trials and tribulations because they have helped me increase my trust factor. Gratitude is essential for living the life I want to live.

Giving thanks, acknowledging the support from your higher self and the Universe is our next Foolproof Step, it's the icing on our manifesting cake.

CHAPTER 8
Foolproof Step #4: Gratitude

"Develop an attitude of gratitude and give thanks for everything that happens to you. Knowing that every step forward is a step toward achieving something bigger and better than your current situation."
—Brian Tracy

Develop an attitude of gratitude. It kind of rolls off the tongue, doesn't it? Develop an attitude of gratitude. What a wonderful thought. Be thankful for ALL that happens to you? Sometimes that may be a stretch.

Looking back on some of the stories I have shared with you, like getting fired from Morgan Stanley or having back surgery ... be thankful for these? Yes, Yes, Yes! What did those seemingly negative experiences bring to me? My return home, back in the love and support of my family and the new spiritual direction that I had desired for many years.

Take a moment to remember some of those dark times in your life. What were the end results? It may be a long-term result, but your result, if you allowed it, probably took you to a much more positive place.

Now, let's look at your day-to-day life. How can gratitude help us create the life we want?

> *"Gratitude opens the door to ... the power, the wisdom, the creativity of the Universe."* —Deepak Chopra

Gratitude may be one of the most overlooked tools, the one people most often forget, when working with the Law of Attraction. Gratitude immediately raises your vibration, so that you connect more completely with the Universe.

One can't manifest more without being appreciative of what they already have. Remember the concept of acceptance? Accept your current situation, whatever it is, then ask for something better. If you can find something you liked even in the worst job, that's also appreciation! Acceptance and appreciation are "kissing cousins," they work very well together.

The benefits of gratitude could fill an entire book. We are going to look at only a few of them, probably the most popular ones. Researchers at Eastern Washington University discovered the #1 benefit of people who experience the most gratitude is feeling a sense of abundance in their lives.

Would you like more abundance?

First, show gratitude for what you already have.

Other studies show gratitude improves physical health (Personality and Individual Differences, 2012), psychological health and self-esteem (Journal of Applied Psychology, 2014) and mental health (Behavior Research and Therapy, 2016). Not bad for simply appreciating what you have, is it?

Gratitude can make you feel happy in the present moment. It also has longer-term "happiness" effects. A study from the University of Pennsylvania in 2013, found that people who personally wrote a thank you note (not an email or tweet) felt happier for a month after sending it. They also found that people who wrote down three positive things each day kept their happiness factor going for up to six months. Impressive, right?

Gratitude is a key step in manifesting while working with the Law of Attraction. Why? When you feel happy, your thoughts and vibrations are higher. These vibrations are released into the Universe and seek other higher vibrations. If you are not thankful for the things you have, you send out negative vibrations and you can't expect to receive positive in return. The Law of Attraction states like attracts like.

Here's a tool that I have adopted with great success. Get yourself a pad or a journal to keep on your nightstand next to your bed. Each night, just before going to sleep, write down one thing you are thankful for that occurred that day. No repeats! Please don't write "my family" every night.

Start with one (build up to three), but if more occur certainly add them as well. This will encourage you to focus on looking for something new to appreciate each day.

Where will your focus be? On the positive.

Where will your thoughts and vibrations be? High!

What will you attract? More things to be thankful for.

Funny how that works. Like attracts like.

Amit Amin, in his article, "Happier Human," writes "A five-minute a day gratitude journal can increase your long-term well-being by more than 10 percent. That's the same impact as doubling your income." Gratitude makes us feel more gratitude.

The gratitude that is produced within those five journaling minutes is enough to trigger a grateful mood. We then feel gratitude more frequently, more intense and for a longer period of time.

As an added benefit to journaling your gratitude just before going to bed, you will drift off to sleep with those wonderful, high-flying feelings and vibrations. Sweet dreams, everyone.

Expressing appreciation is training your brain to look for the positives, which, in turn, keep you learning to be more grateful. Jessica Cassidy, in her article "How to Cultivate and Attitude of Gratitude" coined a term that I love, which is to "Happify" our lives. Look for and appreciate the positives, and "Happify" our lives. Make thank you a habit.

I am coaching a group of clients on the spiritual principles involved with creating abundance, primarily financial abundance. Gratitude plays a major role. We are doing the gratitude journals and taking it a step further to say "thank you" for each check we write while paying our bills. This is a new concept to most. Who is ever happy to be paying out money for mortgage, utilities or especially taxes?

Let's think about that for a moment. We use our money as an exchange for goods and services. We are thanking the electric company for providing our homes with light and in some cases, heat. We pay the mortgage company for a place to live and even taxes for police protection, garbage pickup and many more needed services. So why not appreciate the exchange?

I have started to always write "thank you" in the memo section of my checks and say aloud "thank you" to my computer when paying online. It's all about the energy you are transmitting out to the Universe.

You must pay these bills anyway, why not pay them with gratitude? Never miss an opportunity to show your appreciation. You will be handsomely rewarded with the Law of Attraction.

Well, we are now well into manifesting the life we want. Let's review. So far, we have learned the first four Foolproof steps in creating the life you want:

1. Clarity and Focus
2. The Universal Laws of Attraction, Deliberate Creation, Allowing and Detachment
3. Trust
4. Gratitude

We now have the tools, but how to use them?

We have the ingredients in our creating mixing bowl. How to proceed?

It's now time to step up and become partners with your higher self and the Universe (alignment) and get crackin' (momentum).

Our final Foolproof Step is Alignment-Momentum. Next chapter, please ...

CHAPTER 9
Foolproof Step #5: Alignment–Momentum

"Life's like a bicycle. To keep your
balance, you must keep moving."
—Abraham-Hicks

I will be forever grateful to my coach, mentor and friend, Christy Whitman, for introducing me to the process of Alignment–Momentum. In fact, during our mentor calls, she would have me repeat "Alignment-Momentum" so many times it soon became my mantra. Those two words changed my life.

I have always been a go-getter, a force to be reckoned with, working harder than anyone around me. One time I had a boss tell me, "Cathy, your half-ass effort still beats the rest of the office." Yes, I was a hard worker, but not always a smart worker. Ever heard of the phrase, "Work smarter, not harder?"

Ever had a goal that you worked your butt off to accomplish, but it seemed like real drudgery?

Felt like you were pushing a giant boulder up a mountain?

More often than not, that was me. I accomplished things by sheer force, determination and drive, all by myself. The only problem was that I was completely drained all the time. I hated the journey, couldn't wait for it to be over. It was no fun at all. I may have been creating, but totally on my own, without my creative partner, the Universe. When Christy introduced me to the Alignment-Momentum philosophy, the light came on ... another Aha! moment.

Alignment means support, creating a partnership, straight-line order, structure to improve results. These are all assets to have with you when you are striving for goals. I am suggesting you align with your higher self (your Source, inner being) and then send out your intention to the Universe, your creative partner. Don't leave 50 percent of your creating team out in the cold. Join forces with your Source and the Universe by aligning with them first.

Aligning with your higher self is different for everyone. However, here are some common feelings: your heart feels open and your body feels in tune with your goal (intention). Sometimes you may feel extra confident, a sense of well-being, a light airy sensation with sparks of creativity shooting out. You may feel "in the zone." You feel on purpose, on track, going in the right direction. Who wouldn't want to feel like that?

I'd like to share with you how I get into alignment. Before each presentation, writing, or any task including coaching, I take a few deep breaths, and visualize my heart opening ... kind of like a flower opening. I usually think of a rose (that was my Mom's favorite flower), and speak to my inner self and the Universe (sometimes to myself, sometimes out loud). I say, "Please speak through me ... so that I may accomplish _____ (my intention). Help me to be confident, compassionate, knowledgeable and feel that I am doing all that I can do to serve. When I have successfully accomplished _____ (whatever the task), I want to feel that I nailed it, and did my best work." Then, and only then, do I begin moving forward with my action. It takes only a minute or two and the burst of energy, confidence and "you got this" feeling is awesome.

You need to take that moment to ask for help and support. The Universe is patiently waiting for your call, as it doesn't just jump in and take over. That's not its job. You ask ... it answers. You have the free will to make the choice to co-create or take it all on your shoulders, like I used to do.

Let's take a short break from reading right now.

Yep, right now.

You are going to get into alignment.

Please take in a few deep breaths, close your eyes and ask to connect with your higher self. You may start to feel a sense of peace and relaxation, knowing that you no longer have to do it all alone. Visualize whatever helps you feel that way (this is where I see Mom's rose blooming). When you feel at ease, tell the Universe what you want to co-create (your intention). You are now in alignment.

Remember, practice makes perfect. Each time you get into alignment, it becomes easier. Soon it will be second nature. Be open to what thoughts, feelings or ideas may come. If those insights feel good, start the momentum.

Momentum means moving forward. This is where we may have a bit of trouble. Momentum is taking action—doing something—it doesn't even have to be directly related to what you want to manifest. Just take some action—some forward movement, so that the Universe knows you are serious about your intention. It can then start giving you inspired thoughts, sending opportunities and people in your path to help you along the way.

Let's say your intention is to find a new and loving relationship. If you just sit there in alignment, like a guru or monk on a mountaintop ... you'll feel great, sitting there in your saffron robes ... BUT you'll never find that relationship because there is no action. You probably will not enter a relationship, unless you want to start something with the mailman who comes to your door each day.

What can you do to take action? Maybe go out with friends or join a group that you have a passion for, so you are focusing on the passion not desperately seeking a mate.

When I was in college, a close friend of mine was a theater major. She had this crush on a guy who was into computers, a real tech genius. She even joined the

Computer Club to spend time with him. She didn't understand a thing they discussed at the meetings and had absolutely no interest in computers. However, being an actress, it was fun watching her act out her experiences.

Joining a club that was a total bore to her was not one of her best decisions. She didn't get the guy, and quit the club as soon as she realized her fantasy boyfriend already had a girlfriend. So, when you start working with momentum, join a group that you are excited about and have a real interest in, not in desperation to find a boyfriend or girlfriend.

To manifest, first align, state your request, ask the Universe for help and support and second, take some positive action.

Some of us have trouble with that action step. We are great at getting ready, we think we have it all together—Alignment and Ready for action! The Universe says, okay, let's go. I am here and ready to support you. Let's get started!

But, we seem to be stuck. Oh yeah, we talk a good game but, we seem to be in a state of "Fixin' To." Maybe we are scared, needing to have more prep time or research. Maybe we don't feel worthy or confident or deserving—whatever the reason—so we stay in a state of "Fixin' To."

Please let me explain: "fixin' to" is a southern term. If any of you are from the South, I apologize if I offend you, because "fixin' to" is not one of my favorite phrases.

I'd like to share with you a story about how I came upon this phrase, "fixin' to."

About twenty years ago, when I was living in New York City, my oldest daughter, Andrea, was married to a Southern boy from Alabama. I would go down to visit them every chance I got. I remember one summer visit sitting on one of their friend's front porch. We were enjoying the summer day, sitting in rocking chairs each with a glass of delicious sweet tea.

We were all rocking and enjoying each other's company when Andrea's friend's wife poked her head out the screen door and asked her husband, "Are you going to cut the grass today?" He smiled and replied, "Honey, I'm fixin' to."

We all returned to our conversation and our sweet tea. About a half hour later, the wife returned with the same request, now with a tinge of anger in her voice, as she again asked, "HONEY ... WHAT ABOUT THE GRASS!" Once again, her husband replied, "HONEY, I told you I'm FIXIN' TO!"

Do you think the grass got cut that day?

You see, the husband was in alignment with the beautiful day and having fun spending time and conversation with all his guests. And maybe he had the intention to cut the grass ... but where was the Momentum or Action? It was non-existent at that moment.

When you set your intention, and align with the Universe, what do you do next?

Are you moving forward or still rocking on the porch? It's important to take time to rest and enjoy life ... but not when it's time for taking action.

Please remember this "hangin' out, rocking chair" visual when you feel stuck or unable to move forward for whatever reason. Decide, is this the time for relaxation? Or is this the time to kick butt and move forward? The Universe is ready, willing and able to support you in manifesting your dreams. Are you ready and committed to take that first action step?

If so, right now, set an intention for something you want to manifest. Choose whatever you want. Then take a piece of paper and number it ...

1.

2.

3.

Write down three action steps you are committed to take this week to start and continue that momentum. The Universe is waiting.

Are you ready?

Once you start taking action, moving forward, practicing momentum, that's when the Universe adds the inspired thoughts and ideas, and you are off to manifesting-land.

How do you know if what you're receiving "idea-wise" is from the Universe?

The Universe offers inspired thoughts and ideas, support that easily brings results and leads you to move closer to your intention. Remember that boulder I was always pushing up the mountain? An inspired idea from the Universe would feel like that boulder was rolling down the mountain, rather than having to push it up. The actions are fun, easy and seem like child's play.

Take a gut check, when you are taking the action. How does it feel? If it feels good, I'll bet it is coming from the Universe. If it feels bad, straining to push that boulder up the mountain, it's probably coming from somewhere else.

Discovering your action is not inspired is okay as it is offering you an opportunity to course correct. As I previously mentioned, there is no failure, only feedback to allow you to get back on track.

As you become more comfortable working with the Universe, you will know very quickly when you are starting to veer off course by how you feel. Intuition or gut instinct is real.

I have been telling my family for the past three years that I am going to write a book. Last Christmas, my daughter, Christine gave me a beautiful journal with the inscription, "Notes for your upcoming book." It was finally time to take action. I had been setting my intention for a long time, but that's as far as I got. Completely without momentum. One day a few months ago, I decided to write down all my ideas for the book's content in my new journal.

Within days, I started receiving emails from selfpublishingschool.com with the subject, "How to stop procrastinating and start writing." Talk about timing! I signed up immediately. Now here we are. I acted and the ideas just flowed. Thank you, Universe!

The project was fun, creative and absolutely like child's play. Each day I looked forward to writing the next chapter. Now I feel such fulfillment, joy and gratitude that so many people are benefiting from my Alignment-Momentum.

I like to think of Alignment-Momentum as a baseball team. Alignment is the pitcher and Momentum is the batter. Alignment throws the pitch—but if the batter doesn't swing (if he's "fixin' to") nothing happens, right? But, if the batter is ready, confident, all systems go attitude, and swings ... the ball can be hit out the park. Alignment-Momentum, they are a team. You, your higher self and the Universe are in charge of your manifesting team.

We can all live the lives we want, and have fun during the journey, thanks to Christy Whitman's manifestation equation.

Clarity + Alignment + Action = Manifestation

Get clear on what you want. Get into alignment with your higher self and the Universe then move forward.

Sometimes moving forward is not so easy, because moving forward means change.

Do you embrace change or resist it? Your attitude can make the difference between change being an ordeal or an adventure.

What's your attitude concerning change?

CHAPTER 10
Embracing Change

"Life is change. Growth is optional.
Choose wisely."
—Karen Kaiser Clark

Change is one of those scary words starting with "C" (like Cancer). Sooner or later we all deal with the big "C" (Change). We can resist it or embrace it. Either way, it still comes, again and again.

In creating the life we want, we want change. We have already set our intention for change. Even though we want it, we may still resist it.

Why resist something we have asked for?

It may seem simple minded, but we resist change because we fear loss of control. We fear sharing our creative powers with the Universe. We need to continue to develop Trust with our higher power and the Universe.

There is temporary uncertainty because things seem different, not like they used to be. We may not be happy with where we are, but ... there is fear of what might be coming. The unknown can be a powerful deterrent to stepping forward. It can also be the old "am I ready, can I really do this?" syndrome.

These feelings of uncertainty, fear and resistance can throw up roadblocks to your momentum.

How to move forward?

Take a step back ... re-answer those three questions from Chapter 4:

1. What do I want?
2. Why do I want it?
3. How will I feel when I have it?

Then, take baby steps!

Focus on the reason why you set your intention for this desired change and feel the essence of how you are going to feel. Focus on the feeling, the baby steps will come.

Here's a fun and kind of simple example of my recent "forced" change concerning grocery shopping.

I moved back to Ohio in 2008. Settling in my new home, I needed to find all the necessities; doctor, vet, shopping mall and yes, a grocery store.

I decided on Giant Eagle. Located about five minutes away, with all the bells and whistles, plus FREE gas points. I love free gas! Grocery shopping has never been a favorite past time; it's been a chore to be completed. I did not pay a lot of attention to seeking out the best option. Giant Eagle was the closest, so it was my choice.

So, for the past eight years, I made my weekly trek to that grocery store. As years passed, the store began to decline. They no longer carried some of the products I liked and the service seemed to be trending downhill. It became a common joke to bet on which cashier was the slowest, while standing in the checkout line.

There was a Kroger's grocery store about two miles down the street, but I stayed with my Giant Eagle, slowly accepting the negative changes. I was not willing to embrace the thought of trying Kroger's to see if that might be a better option, as many of my friends had suggested. I was resisting. As we know, when we resist, we can't receive.

Lo and behold in January of this year, a news story broke that my Giant Eagle was closing. The pharmacy would be closing in late January and the store following in early March. Such a minor change in the whole scheme of life, but it got to me. I hated to think about it.

In January, I was forced to change pharmacies. I picked the Kroger's, two miles down the street, as they too had a drive thru service—but it was different! I continued to shop at my Giant Eagle, complaining the whole time, still resisting the upcoming closure.

Finally, in late February, I decided to embrace my situation and investigate Kroger's. I felt a bit intimidated, not knowing where anything was located. Kroger's was twice the size of my tried and true grocery.

As I entered the huge store, I must have looked slightly apprehensive as a lady in produce came right over, smiled, and said, "Welcome to Kroger's, how may I help you?"

That friendly employee helped break the ice. I started to walk around to get my bearings. I discovered that Kroger's had so much more produce, beautifully arranged and many of my favorites that were no longer at Giant Eagle.

It took a few visits, but now I love it. I shake my head and think, "Why did you wait so long? Why did you resist this wonderful new opportunity?"

By finally embracing my grocery change, I look forward to food shopping. With all the new choices now available to me, I think of it as a fun adventure. As I embraced the change, I received so many new options.

My grocery change may seem very elementary to most life changes, but the principle is the same. Embrace Change!

Here are some tips to help you reduce your resistance and move forward.

Take baby steps. You don't need to jump into the deep end; dip your toes in first, then slowly wade into the pool. It's your journey, take the size steps that make you feel comfortable. Remember, first the parking space before the lottery win.

Reduce your expectations and detach from the result. Keep your eye on the prize (your intention) and release the *how* and *when* to the Universe.

Think of change as an opportunity rather than the enemy. Those butterflies in your stomach feel pretty much the same for fear and resistance as they do for anticipation and excitement. Focus on the positive, release the negative. Zig Ziglar, well-known author and motivational speaker used to say, "Get rid of that stinkin' thinkin'." Start looking forward to becoming your "new you."

Learn from experience. Take a moment to review your past changes. How have you grown from them? You survived and expanded. Why wouldn't this change be the same?

Think of change as the air going into a balloon. The more air that goes in, the higher the balloon can fly. I like to visualize a big red balloon soaring high into the sky. With each change, we grow stronger, we fly a little higher.

Life Coach, Andrea Schulman says, "Change is the Universe's way of preparing you for something you've been wanting."

I have experienced many changes in my life (as we all have) such as various careers, divorce and parents transitioning. With each change, lessons have been learned, clarity gained, and momentum ignited.

In the words of experienced photographer and yoga teacher, Rachel Wolchin, "If we were meant to stay in one place, we'd have roots instead of feet." We are the kind of beautiful flower that grows wherever we are planted, and we are replanted quite often.

Now that we are embracing change, moving forward with the Universe, focusing on our clear intention, while working with the Law of Attraction, we need to double check that our intentions are going to truly fulfill our authentic self. Are we pleasing who we really are, or trying to makes others happy?

Who is our true authentic self?

CHAPTER 11
Be Your Authentic Self

"To thine own self be true."
—William Shakespeare

Who am I? Am I living my true, authentic life?

Authenticity is something that is easier said than done. We all want to be true to ourselves, because that's the way to happiness, right? Yes, it is the way to *lasting* happiness.

Then why is it so hard to live authentic lives? Because, we often don't know who we are deep down inside.

We have all been programmed by our parents, care givers, teachers, friends and even the media how to behave, how to be successful, how to be liked and fit in. During all that programming, we may have lost our true selves.

I was the go-getter, striving for good grades to feel valued by my parents. I was the high producer to feel valued by my bosses. I was finding my value in pleasing others. But concerning my true self, I didn't have a clue until later in life. I now realize finding my authentic self is a journey, a wonderful and continuous life journey.

Who is your authentic self? Michael Eisen, in his article, "Living the Authentic You," writes, "To be your authentic self is to be in a space of alignment where everything you say and do feels right ... you will often feel comfortable, secure, loved, understood and at ease." Dr. Phil adds, "It's the real, true, genuine substance of who you are, not defined by your job, function or role."

You are living authentically when you are rooted in your deepest beliefs and values. Living for yourself, not to please others. We can then enjoy a new sense of freedom. It takes courage and commitment to discover and live your authentic life. So, how do we get there?

I'd like to share a process I experienced a few years ago. It's opened my eyes to finding my true me. I discovered my WHY. First, I discovered Ridgely Goldsborough, best-selling author, international speaker and co-founder of the "Know Your Why" program (knowyourwhy.com). Actually, Christy Whitman introduced us.

Christy had completed her WHY process, learned that Ridgely was recruiting coaches to join his program and suggested my name. The Universe was offering an opportunity once again as I had set my intention to add more tools to my coaching practice.

Ridgely guided me into my WHY by asking me to share a few stories from my life where I felt successful. I was amazed at the accuracy and depth of the result. The entire process took about twenty minutes. My WHY is "To Create Relationships Based on Trust." Trust flows through all phases of my life.

Let me further explain the WHY concept, from *The WHY Engine*, by Ridgely Goldsborough. Your WHY is your roots, your true authentic self. It's why you make the decisions you make, how you think, what you believe, it's how you are hard-wired. It's what makes you unique and it's what people can count on you for. It's the cornerstone of your authentic self.

When you know your WHY, your life makes sense and you better understand yourself and others. With self-understanding comes the clarity and confidence to move forward creating the life you want. You are building a strong foundation.

Ridgely writes, "Without knowing why you exist, you fall victim to the circumstances around you and never define life on your own terms."

Your WHY began to develop when you were an infant. When you were a wee little one, and you needed something (formula or milk), you would cry and your mom or dad would come running, catering to all your needs. You soon learned that crying equals success.

That crying worked great for a while until Mom and Dad stopped being at your beck and call (usually at toddler age). So, what then? How do you get your needs filled? You started to try different things to bring back that success. It was hit or miss until you hit on something that worked, something that brought you the same level of success that crying used to bring. You kept on repeating that behavior because it kept bringing you what you wanted, it brought you success. That behavior is your WHY.

Your WHY is just like the Law of Attraction. Whether you know your WHY or not, it still runs everything that you do. It's like a filter through which you see the world. Once you know your WHY, you understand yourself and can bring clarity to how you want your world to unfold. You become empowered.

Knowing my WHY has brought peace, and a real understanding of my authentic self. As I previously mentioned, my WHY is "Creating Relationships Based on Trust." Some of my characteristics include trust being the driving force behind all I stand for and is certainly needed in teaching, selling and coaching. I will go out of my way to work long hours, overproduce to prove I can be trusted, and go to great lengths to become highly educated in a particular area, having received my Masters in Business Administration. All to demonstrate expertise in establishing trust. Trust-oriented people are approachable, set goals, are leaders, not afraid of accountability and like recognition. And ... they are usually animal lovers. The Trust WHY has me pegged.

Uncovering my WHY has given me many insights into my past decisions and behaviors. During my dating years, before marriage and after divorce, whenever a relationship ended, it was totally over. I was never able to remain friends after a break up. I remember feeling there must be something was wrong with me as many of my friends followed their break ups with a platonic relationship with their exes. Now I understand. For me, when the trust is gone from a relationship, the end is here ... no friends, it's over! That's just the way I am, and that's okay.

Being an animal lover is in my DNA. Where else can you find total trust and unconditional love? My pets have always been there for me. There is a special trusting bond between my collies and me. I know a lot of you animal lovers can relate to that.

Now that I understand the prominent role trust plays in my life, I am able to be very particular in choosing people to work with. I feel comfortable in my own skin and can quickly pick up on untrusting situations. The clarity and self-acceptance that knowing my WHY has brought me is like a light coming on ... another Aha! moment.

There are 9 WHYS, each with their own characteristics. What makes each of us unique is how we bring these characteristics to life. The discovery process is simple and fun, and takes only about twenty minutes. If you would like to learn more about discovering your WHY and receive a five-chapter excerpt of Ridgely Goldsborough's best-selling book, *The WHY Engine*, plus the bonus of my weekly newsletter, "Happy Thoughts Thursday," all free, please visit http://lifecoachingbycathy.com/free-gifts/.

Now we have completed the five Foolproof steps to creating the life you want:

1. Clarity and Focus
2. The Laws of Attraction, Deliberate Creation, Allowing and Detachment
3. Trust
4. Gratitude
5. Alignment-Momentum
   AND THE BONUS ... Be Your Authentic Self

You have all the tools you need to start creating. One final word of advice as you continue your journey. Lighten up! Life is supposed to be fun. You don't have to struggle all the time. My motto used to be "No Pain, No Gain." Since I was focusing on Pain (the Universe doesn't distinguish if there is a "no" before the focus word), guess what I attracted?

Let's focus on FUN, making our new mantra, "Remember What's Important and Have Fun!" That refocusing made quite a difference in my life as you will see in the next chapter.

CHAPTER 12
Remember What's Important and Have Fun

"Please don't worry. I've got your back."
—The Universe

When I first began working with the Law of Attraction, I was dead serious. Having grown up with Dad's work ethic, I was functioning in the theory, "No Pain, No Gain." Being so serious didn't allow much time for fun. I needed to lighten up.

As we are creating our life, we have the choice to work ourselves to the bone and get there worn out, stressed and exhausted or we can focus and partner with the Universe while having a ball enjoying the ride.

How does your life look?

Are you seeking the silver lining in your challenges?

Looking for fun and adventure in your journey?

Are the thoughts and vibrations you are sending out filled with fun and excitement or stress and frustration?

You can still be wildly successful creating your awesome life while having fun.

I learned this lesson just in the nick of time for my daughter Christine's wedding. May 28, 2016, was a wonderful blessed day for my family. It was Christine's wedding day. This was a blending of families as Christine had two teenage sons, Kaesyn and Maguire and Jeff, the groom, had a cute little guy, five-year-old Mason.

Both Jeff and Christine wanted a small, simple, low key, outdoor wedding with just family and a few friends. It ended up being a bit larger than first planned (about eighty guests) as well as a bit more stressful than we had planned.

Christine always has wonderful, creative ideas, including stringing tiny white lights wrapped in pink tulle (that's a netting-like fabric, for you guys) in the peaks of the twenty-foot tall tent and running down to the edges. The idea was fabulous ... but doable?

Ordering the caterers, flowers and cartoonist (to gift each guest with a cute family portrait), became a very stressful situation for me. Then, throw in the weather as the ceremony was to be performed in the garden—my blood pressure and stress level continued to rise.

Everybody kept telling me it looks like rain that day. After awhile, they stopped as I gave them the evil eye, saying (sometimes yelling), "It's gonna be fine! I set my intention for clear skies." I was beginning to allow this wonderful event to become filled with contrast, negativity and stress.

I was in the process of completing my certification in Hypnotherapy at that time so I asked my "Hypno Coaching Buddy" to give me a session to reduce my stress.

All I can say is it was amazing! I fell into a deeply relaxed state as we talked about what was really bothering me, and what was really important to me. I was then guided back to a peaceful day in my life where I was happy, calm and content.

I went back to a trip that Christine and I had taken over twenty years ago to Puerto Rico. We were enjoying the beach, the sunshine, listening to the waves and seagulls. All was well. All was lovely and peaceful. I was asked to bring back a thought, phrase or feeling to anchor in that calm, peaceful and stress free experience. I was then instructed to put my index finger and thumb together (like the "okay" sign) and deeply feel that wonderful relaxing, stress free, feeling. The phrase that came to me was, "Remember What's Important ... and Have Fun."

As the wedding drew closer, and I began to feel the stress coming on, I took a deep breath and used my phrase, "Remember What's Important ... and Have Fun," while placing my index finger and thumb together (and feeling a-okay).

People were running around, sometimes nearly out of control, and I just smiled and flashed my anchor sign, going back to the stress-free Puerto Rico beach, "Remembering What's Important ... and Having Fun".

What a difference my little anchor made! The wedding day preparations were completed, including the groom climbing up a twenty foot ladder to hang the lights and tulle in the tent. The rain which fell on and off until five minutes before the ceremony stopped right on time, cooling off the humidity and ushering in a beautiful dry evening. The food and desserts were delicious and the cartoonist was a big hit. The ceremony was beautiful and so was our bride. Everyone had fun, especially me.

With all the hustle and bustle, in our lives, we often need to take time to "Remember What's Important" and, always, always, "To Have Fun."

Remember that old reggae song, "Don't Worry, Be Happy"? That's a much better motto than "No Pain, No Gain."

Happiness is when your life fulfills your needs. It's a feeling of contentment, just like finding your authentic self, and fulfilling your life's journey. You are never too young or too old to start as proven by this following heart warming post I found on Facebook a few years ago. I have saved it so every now and then I can read it again. The story originally was posted on December 8, 2013 by the page "Just Eat Real Food." This is the story of a lovely ninety-two-year-old, petite, well-poised and proud lady who is fully dressed each morning by eight o'clock, with her hair fashionably coifed and makeup perfectly applied.

Our pretty lady is legally blind and is moving into a nursing home today. Her husband of seventy years recently passed away, making the move necessary. After many hours of waiting patiently in the lobby of the nursing home, she smiled sweetly when told her room was ready. As she maneuvered her walker to the elevator, the nurse provided a visual description of her tiny room, including the eyelet sheets that had been hung on her window.

"I love it," she stated with the enthusiasm of an eight-year-old having just been presented with a new puppy. "Mrs. Jones, you haven't seen the room, just wait." "That doesn't have anything to do with it," Mrs. Jones replied. "Happiness is something you decide on ahead of time."

She continued, "Whether I like my room or not doesn't depend on how the furniture is arranged, it's how I arrange my mind. I already decided to love it. It's a decision I make every morning when I wake up. I have a choice; I can spend the day in bed recounting the difficulty I have with the parts of my body that no longer work, or get out of bed and be thankful for the ones that do. Each day is a gift, and as long as my eyes open I'll focus on the new day and all the happy memories I've stored away, just for this time in my life." She went on to explain, "Old age is like a bank account, you withdraw from what you've put in. So, my advice to you would be to deposit a lot of happiness in your bank account of memories." Then she said with a smile, "Thank you for your part in filling my Memory bank today. I am still depositing."

Are you depositing many, many wonderful memories to your "bank account"? Are you ready to create the life you want to increase those memory deposits?

All Ya Gotta Do is ... ACT, Align-Connect-Transform.

One final quote from Abraham-Hicks: "Being happy is the cornerstone of all that you are! Nothing is more important than that you feel good! And you have absolute and utter control about that because you can choose the thought that makes you worry or the thought that makes you happy; the things that thrill you, or the things that worry you. You have the choice in every moment."

It's your choice. We have now come to the end of my book and the beginning of your journey.

If you didn't get your FREE GIFTS at the beginning of my book, here's another opportunity to receive your subscription to "Happy Thoughts Thursday", a relaxing and rewarding Manifesting Abundance Meditation and a summary report on the 7 Universal Laws. Please click below:
http://lifecoachingbycathy.com/book-free-gifts/

Thank you so very much. My deepest appreciation for taking this journey with me. Please enjoy your gifts!

If I may be of service as you create the life you want, I would be honored to offer my guidance. Feel free to contact me at:

http://lifecoachingbycathy.com/

Until we meet again,

"Let's Transform Lives Together"

Love,

Cathy

MEET THE AUTHOR

 Cathy Brown is a Certified Law of Attraction Life Coach, graduate of Awakening Your Light Body, and Energy Mindfulness for Awakening Consciousness. As well, she is a Certified Hypnotherapist, Reiki Master Teacher and Creating Money Coach.

In addition to being an active participant in metaphysical studies for over 30 years, Cathy brings a wealth of business building and entrepreneurial experience to her coaching. She holds a Master's Degree in Business Administration after having developed several successful businesses. Cathy combines the spiritual principles and pragmatic business experience she has learned to develop a unique perspective for client transformation.

Cathy has a compassionate, fun, humorous and down to earth writing and coaching style. This provides her with the ability to break down challenging concepts into bite-size understandable pieces so you can use them in your everyday life. She is a knowing teacher, a trusted mentor/coach and a believer in miracles.

Cathy offers personal coaching sessions, business mentoring, online group classes and is a "Know Your WHY" facilitator. She has personally experienced the wonders of the Universal Laws and is truly honored to share them with you.

You may contact Cathy at Cathy@lifecoachingbycathy.com or visit her website http://lifecoachingbycathy.com

Made in the USA
Lexington, KY
05 March 2018